D0154256

Marc E. Vargo, MS

Scandal
Infamous Gay Controversies of the Twentieth Century

*Pre-publication
REVIEWS,
COMMENTARIES,
EVALUATIONS . . .*

"**A**n English novelist, an Irish patriot, a German general, a Cuban poet, an Italian filmmaker, two English spies, and a South African activist all found themselves involved in scandals in which their homosexuality was trumpeted to the press or brought out in a court trial, even when their same-sex preference had little to do with the issues. Marc Vargo tells their stories, and reminds us all just how hazardous it was in the recent past to be labeled as gay or lesbian, and how homosexuality is sensationalized in the media to the detriment of the individuals involved. It makes for fascinating reading as well as leaving one fearful that such incidents still occur."

Vern L Bullough, RN, PhD
SUNY Distinguished Professor
Emeritus; Visiting Professor,
University of Southern California,
Los Angeles; Editor, *Before Stonewall:
Activists for Gay and Lesbian Rights
in Historical Context*

"**S**trong and persuasive, Marc E. Vargo provides us with seven major and controversial episodes from modern twentieth-century history in which gays and lesbians prominently figure. One is astounded by the scope of *Scandal*, ranging across continents and countries along all levels of society and areas in which the central figures are involved, from literature to films to politics.

Scandals are not generally a result of the homosexuality of the leading players, but rather of how the gay lives of the various men and women came to influence the outcome of the scandal and often overwhelm its other, more important aspects. Just as gay men and women have contributed so much to worldwide culture and history, so has their presence been a crucial part of the more fascinating and controversial aspects of modern history."

Anthony Slide
Historian; Author, *Lost Gay Novels:
A Reference Guide to Fifty Works from
the First Half of the Twentieth Century*
and *Gay and Lesbian Characters
and Themes in Mystery Novels*

CONCORDIA UNIVERSITY LIBRARY
PORTLAND, OR 97211

More pre-publication
REVIEWS, COMMENTARIES, EVALUATIONS . . .

"Marc Vargo's retelling of famous court cases takes his readers around the globe and to specific moments in history, as far back as World War I and as recent as the 1980s. Passionately written and carefully researched, *Scandal* should appeal to anyone interested in the history of gay rights and the impact of the media and judicial system on the public's perception of homosexuality. Whether they were accused of espionage or obscenity, all of Vargo's subjects faced the wrath of the judicial system, media, and general public, not because of their activism or art, but because of their sexuality.

Each chapter stands on its own, but ultimately connecting these diverse cases are their tragic conclusions. Although they may have hoped that the scandals surrounding their work or private lives would lead to greater public aware-ness and tolerance for homosexuality, Vargo's subjects were instead punished by means as varied as book banning, murder, imprisonment, and psychological and physical illness.

What makes Vargo's study especially intriguing is that his cases involve gay heroes as well as villains, and artists whose work ranges from tame to deliberately pornographic. Their public lives and art have been buried by scandal; now remembered only for their refusal to conform to society's sexual codes, Vargo's subjects expose the lie behind Pasolini's claim that 'to be scandalized is a pleasure.'"

Julie Anne Taddeo, PhD
Visiting Scholar,
University of California at Berkeley;
Author, *Lytton Strachey and the Search for Modern Sexual Identity: The Last Eminent Victorian*

Harrington Park Press®
An Imprint of The Haworth Press, Inc.
New York • London • Oxford

NOTES FOR PROFESSIONAL LIBRARIANS AND LIBRARY USERS

This is an original book title published by Harrington Park Press®, an imprint of The Haworth Press, Inc. Unless otherwise noted in specific chapters with attribution, materials in this book have not been previously published elsewhere in any format or language.

CONSERVATION AND PRESERVATION NOTES

All books published by The Haworth Press, Inc. and its imprints are printed on certified pH neutral, acid free book grade paper. This paper meets the minimum requirements of American National Standard for Information Sciences-Permanence of Paper for Printed Material, ANSI Z39.48-1984.

Scandal
Infamous Gay Controversies of the Twentieth Century

HARRINGTON PARK PRESS
New, Recent, and Forthcoming Titles
of Related Interest

Against My Better Judgment: An Intimate Memoir of an Eminent Gay Psychologist by Roger Brown

Rough News—Daring Views: 1950s' Pioneer Gay Press Journalism by Jim Kepner

The Empress Is a Man: Stories from the Life of José Sarria by Michael R. Gorman

Lytton Strachey and the Search for Modern Sexual Identity: The Last Eminent Victorian by Julie Anne Taddeo

From Drags to Riches: The Untold Story of Charles Pierce by John Wallraff

Before Stonewall: Activists for Gay and Lesbian Rights in Historical Context edited by Vern L. Bullough

Lost Gay Novels: A Reference Guide to Fifty Works from the First Half of the Twentieth Century by Anthony Slide

Anything but Straight: Unmasking the Scandals and Lies Behind the Ex-Gay Myth by Wayne R. Besen

Scandal
Infamous Gay Controversies of the Twentieth Century

Marc E. Vargo, MS

HPP

Harrington Park Press®
An Imprint of The Haworth Press, Inc.
New York • London • Oxford

Published by

Harrington Park Press®, an imprint of The Haworth Press, Inc., 10 Alice Street, Binghamton, NY 13904-1580.

© 2003 by Marc E. Vargo. All rights reserved. No part of this work may be reproduced or utilized in any form or by any means, electronic or mechanical, including photocopying, microfilm, and recording, or by any information storage and retrieval system, without permission in writing from the publisher. Printed in the United States of America.

Cover design by Jennifer M. Gaska.

Library of Congress Cataloging-in-Publication Data

Vargo, Marc
    Scandal : infamous gay controversies of the twentieth century / Marc E. Vargo.
       p. cm.
    Includes bibliographical references and index.
    ISBN 1-56023-411-3 (alk. paper)—ISBN 1-56023-412-1 (soft)
    1. Gay men—Case studies. 2. Scandals—Case studies. 3. Homosexuality—Public opinion—History—20th century. I. Title.

HQ76 .V37 2002
305.38'9664—dc21
                                                 2002068533

In memory of my father,
Robert Vargo

Nyugodjék békében

ABOUT THE AUTHOR

Marc E. Vargo, MS, is a staff member in the Psychology Department at Hammond Developmental Center in Hammond, Louisiana. He is the author of *Acts of Disclosure: The Coming-Out Process of Contemporary Gay Men* (Haworth Press), and *The HIV Test: What You Need to Know to Make an Informed Decision.* His work has also appeared in the Italian journal *Cortex,* the *British Journal of Medical Psychology,* and the *Journal of the American Academy of Behavioral Medicine.*

CONTENTS

Foreword

From the age of sixteen, I was almost entirely at ease with the fact of my homosexuality. Reading novels by Alberto Moravia and others such as James Baldwin's *Giovanni's Room,* and John Rechy's *City of Night,* prepared me for a life of brittle glamour, passion, and sadness. In actuality, it has turned out to be much more wholesome and cheerful.

I was a well-informed teenager who had no courage when it came to talking to, or approaching, others. Mentally but not physically brave, I was doomed to six years of enforced celibacy for fear of exposure for a crime that could not even be given a name in the nineteenth century, the crime for which men were hanged, and which, even in twentieth-century Northern Ireland where I lived, made one liable to life imprisonment. I was subject to a level of fear that made it inconceivable to contemplate saying the awful words. I would quicker admit to murder than reveal I was homosexual.

Thus it was that I, a liberal teenager, became very angry at what society had made me deny, and at the result of that denial: lovelessness and sexual emptiness at one's most significantly sexual time. I and others, after we made it through, campaigned, and thereby discovered the "dear love of comrades" within a new gay family—and a noble cause. We, in our twenties, carried on with ordinary lives but did extraordinary things like demonstrating or appearing on TV in Belfast in the middle of a prolonged and bloody civil war. Luckily, our potential tormentors were too busy destroying one another to care, giving us an exclusive run of the city's center at night. Old-timers said there had been nothing like it in Belfast for thirty years, not since the blackout coincided with the arrival of American troops in the days prior to D-Day in 1944.

Then, in 1974, as a member of the Northern Ireland Gay Rights Association, I launched a human rights case against the British government. It took seven years. Before it had hardly started I was subjected to a raid on my house during which the police removed every single piece of paper therein, including the initial documents relating to my case at the European Court of Human Rights in Strasbourg.

Released after a lengthy interrogation, I was awakened a week later in the home, and bed, of my boyfriend Douglas, by the same policemen who had at that time entered upon a long investigation of gay activists in the province. My Canadian boyfriend was also arrested and taken away that morning. Oddly (and with the help of liberal writers in particular), the Belfast gay purges became such an embarrassment that the attorney general in London put a stop to the intended prosecutions, which included Douglas and me (both parties well over the age of twenty-one).

The Strasbourg case was not concluded in my favor until 1981, and it was contested by London every step of the way. A year later the law in Northern Ireland was reformed to that which had applied in England since 1967, although, admittedly, the latter legislation was less than ideal. Still, I had won. *We* had won. I was a reluctant (minor) public figure who appeared on television and received the protection of television fame. Indeed, in December 2000, the British Broadcasting Corporation (BBC) aired a story on the radio about me, the police raids, and the Strasbourg case, so I have become something of a stately homo. Now I assist in training police recruits!

Today in Northern Ireland, out of the peace agreement and the astonishingly, although unremarkable, liberal climate, has come a European first that gives protection in public employment—a statutory duty to produce policy and practice that does not discriminate against gays and lesbians. Things move fast. Twenty-five years ago they wanted to jail me, now my worst problem is being typecast. As a working civil servant I find this new legislation provides great peace of mind and gives me renewed strength where previously I had been slipping back into the closet.

It is, however, a fact to be monotonously observed, that prominent gay men, and to a lesser extent lesbians, invariably hit trouble which may involve bad publicity, the police, and even prison. The list of cases is long and it is being added to, even in these relatively benign times in Europe and North America.

Scandal: Infamous Gay Controversies of the Twentieth Century provides a window into a number of such prominent individuals in recent history who have lived out their homosexual characters, sometimes to excess and oftentimes shockingly. Author Marc E. Vargo provides the reader with a meaty sample of some of those famous, and sometimes infamous, cases of gay controversy and scandal.

Among the angry and marginalized figures found in *Scandal* are Pier Paolo Pasolini and Radclyffe Hall, who have made extraordinary literary careers out of their experiences and feelings. Some, such as Guy Burgess and Donald Maclean (and the anti-American art historian Anthony Blunt) expressed their rage in a distorted manner by committing treason, while others, such as Simon Nkoli, Roger Casement, and Reinaldo Arenas (hero of the recent, highly praised film *Before Night Falls*), honorably rebelled against their countries and/or systems of government. As a result, all these people became vulnerable to the predations of the press and the police, became unintentionally more memorable, and provided the material for many remarkable dramas.

Sadly, there are, and will still be, many other gays and lesbians to write about when it comes to scandal and controversy. Lesser known gay people will continue to feel the lash of the tabloid press—the new high priests who do not offer confession or forgiveness of sins for misdemeanors.

They demand instead higher penalties. Well-known gays may cope better but can still fall from grace, especially if made famous by the media. For instance, the fashionable British singer, George Michael, was caught a couple of years ago allegedly propositioning a plainclothes police officer in California. Such events for ordinary gay people can end in suicide. George Michael had the inner strength to capitalize on it and survive. We all took strength from his unexpected courage.

As Mr. Vargo reveals in this immensely readable volume, the power of scandal actually casts light on areas that might otherwise be invisible or left in such darkness as to be nullified. Documents often survive only because of such difficulties. It has therefore been necessary to revisit gay people's disasters to know how things have come about and how the world has changed. By reading *Scandal,* we will learn of the past that has become our present.

Jeffrey Dudgeon
Belfast, Northern Ireland

Acknowledgments

I deeply appreciate the many people who helped bring this book into existence. They include my agent Pamela Gray Ahearn of the Ahearn Agency, New Orleans; Bill Palmer, Vice President of The Haworth Press book division; and John De Cecco, PhD, Editor in Chief of Haworth's Human Sexuality and Gender Studies program. The production staff was also indispensable, most notably Peg Marr, Ed Medina, Patricia Brown, Marylouise Doyle, and Dawn Krisko. For those on the homefront, suffice it to say this book would not have come about without their kindness and support. They endured my absences and kept me in fine spirits—Michael, Hannah, Missy, and Cornelius—the loves of my life, to whom I will always be grateful.

Introduction

From a truth or from a lie, scandal can emerge and taint everyone involved. Consider the case of Miss Jane Pirie and Miss Marianne Woods, two single women who ran an exclusive girls' school in Edinburgh, Scotland, in the early years of the nineteenth century. One day, without warning, they found themselves the victims of a spiteful young student, Jane Cumming, who decided to wreck their lives by telling her grandmother a lie about them. She said that she had seen the women embrace repeatedly in the middle of the night, stolen moments during which they lifted their nightgowns and caressed one another with "inordinate affection." The grandmother, horrified, notified the authorities at once and within two days the school was shut down. As for Pirie and Woods, they were suddenly at sea, their school ruined, and their reputations in tatters.

The two women, however, refused to be wronged. In the ensuing months, they sued the child's grandmother for libel in what proved to be one of the most scandalous trials in Scottish legal history, scandalous because it dealt with the prospect of same-sex love. Although it was controversial, however, the case did offer potential benefits, not the least of which was that it introduced the subject of lesbianism into public discourse. Unfortunately, the judiciary, as well as the public, were unable to deal with it. Indeed, Lord Meadowbank, the judge hearing the case, simply could not believe that two women could make love.

"Their private parts were not so formed as to penetrate each other," he intoned, "and without penetration . . . orgasm could not possibly follow."[1] In other words, no penis, no sex; truly a male conclusion.

Eventually, the women won their libel claim—on appeal—although they were awarded only a fraction of the damages they sought. Moreover, although they were vindicated by the court, at least in principle, they were haunted by the scandal for the rest of their lives. As for Scottish society, single women who taught in private girls' schools, particularly if they were older, were thereafter viewed with suspicion, as were close relationships between women in general. The controversy did not end there.

A century later, in 1934, author Lillian Hellman wrote a play called *The Children's Hour* based on the Pirie-Woods incident, a play, it turns out, that was banned in London and Chicago due to its allegedly risqué content, despite the fact that the work did not contain the word lesbian or depict, in any form, same-sex love. The play did run in Manhattan, however, where Hellman, in an interview with *The New York Times,* insisted that the play was about lies, not about lesbianism.

In 1936, *The Children's Hour* was made into a film called *These Three,* which starred Merle Oberon, but the producers, hoping to avoid a scandal, transformed a key female role into a male role, thereby purging the homosexual element altogether. Then, in 1962, the play was remade as *The Children's Hour,* this time starring Audrey Hepburn and Shirley MacLaine, and was based on a script that was more faithful to the original case. As before, however, lesbianism was not mentioned in this newer version, nor did the actresses talk about it on the set. Apparently, same-sex love was still too taboo for frank discussion. This, unfortunately, has been the case for several centuries in the Western world, with homosexuality, male or female, considered deserving of moral judgment and its public exposure all too often sparking social and political conflict.

In *Scandal: Infamous Gay Controversies of the Twentieth Century,* we examine seven scandals that erupted in different parts of the world and at different moments during the past century, all of them centering on gay men and lesbians. The controversies range from accusations of obscenity and libel to espionage and political dissent. In nearly every case, had the central players been heterosexual, the scandals would never have occurred, or, had they taken place, they would have been far less sensational. Certainly, most of them would not have made international news.

In addition to recounting the disputes, *Scandal* looks at the legal consequences for the hapless men and women ensnared by these events, penalties that included censorship, imprisonment, deportation, and death. It examines the personal cost too, most notably, the illnesses and social ostracism these individuals suffered. It explores the conflicts' societal fallout, and aftermath that was invariably harsh. Indeed, because these scandals brought the subject of homosexuality into public view in such an explosive manner, and thus rather traumatically, the controversies reversed, or at least stalled, any progress that the gay and lesbian citizenry had made up to that point. Only two of the seven conflicts produced beneficial results for gay men and women, and then only several years later.

Alongside these adverse features, *Scandal* also provides detailed accounts of those intrepid individuals at the heart of the disputes; people who, in most cases, handled themselves admirably. Although none intentionally invited the public trouncing to which they were subjected, several managed the ordeals in such a way as to minimize their damage and maximize their value for the gay and lesbian citizenry.

Ultimately, *Scandal* takes the reader on an intriguing journey through a remarkable collection of same-sex incidents, depicts situations that help us understand how and why such episodes erupt, and illustrates the dignity, courage, and wisdom of a unique handful of gay men and women who struggled nobly to cope with sweeping public condemnation in their day.

Chapter 1

A Trial for Treason:
Roger Casement
and the *Black Diaries*

In the spring of 1916, an Irishman named Sir Roger Casement—former British consul, human rights activist, poet, and gay man—was charged with high treason and confined to the Tower of London to await execution. He was indicted for his role in a conspiracy by Irish freedom fighters to oppose British rule. The decision to put an end to his life did not sit well with the public, his revolutionary leanings notwithstanding. Because Casement was an illustrious gentleman admired the world over for his compassion and integrity, a man who, not long before, had been knighted for his success in protecting native peoples from exploitation and persecution, the verdict shocked the citizenry and triggered an avalanche of protests.

At once, scores of prominent men and women, such as the Archbishop of Canterbury, writers Bernard Shaw, T. E. Lawrence, and Sir Arthur Conan Doyle, set out to secure a pardon for the doomed dignitary. Even the United States senate became involved, formally requesting that King George V consider a stay of execution. All appeals for a reprieve, however, were rejected. On August 3, the statesman was marched, hands bound behind his back, to the scaffold at London's Pentonville Prison and hanged. Said the priest who escorted him on this final walk, Casement moved "with the dignity of a prince and towered straight over us all."[1] Certainly he did, by all accounts, seem to be at peace, which is perhaps understandable given that shortly before his death he explained to a friend that he had long ago reconciled himself to his past and to his fate, and was thus prepared to die.

"I have made awful mistakes," Casement said, "and did heaps of things wrong and failed at much." He added, however, that while some of his deeds may have been misguided, they all had been well intentioned, and that "the best thing was the Congo."[2]

His mention of this region of sub-Saharan Africa was a reference to the humanitarian work he had carried out while on assignment there, a series of courageous tasks he had performed on behalf of beleaguered natives. Yet, it was also his behavior in Africa and later South America—namely, his sexual liaisons with the local men—that, once discovered by the British government through his personal diaries, helped steer him to the gallows in what was to become an enduring scandal in both Ireland and England.

THE CONGO

Casement came to be situated in Africa by the British government, which, in 1903, dispatched him to the faraway reaches of the Congo to investigate suspicions of atrocities. The crimes were allegedly being committed by Belgian forces that had gone to jungles for reasons of greed.

For several centuries, it seems, Europeans had considered the "Dark Continent," as they called it, a place of mystery and peril. But in the late 1800s, it also became the site of political conflict when a handful of European nations began competing for the gold, diamonds, rubber, and human resources—labor forces, to be precise—that Western explorers had discovered there. The undisputed pacesetter in this stampede was King Leopold II of Belgium, a Machiavellian leader who set out to assimilate a large region of Africa as a means of expanding his small nation's boundaries and influence.

Leopold, described as a tall, commanding man with an enormous beard and a nose to match, was among the most despised kings in Europe, a man known for his "cunning intelligence . . . overweening ambition, and personal ruthlessness."[3] Side by side with his hunger for wealth and power, moreover, were his "keenly developed tastes for the pleasures of the flesh."[4] As to his taste for colonization, Leopold made it clear to anyone who would listen that he believed expansionist policies were essential to a robust nation.

"Since history teaches that colonies are useful, that they play a great part in that which makes up the power and prosperity of states," he declared, "let us strive to get one in our turn."[5]

The government of Belgium, however, did not agree. It had no interest in establishing a colony in the Congo or anywhere else, believing the whole notion to be both unnecessary and costly, and so refused to allow Leopold to proceed. The government had the power to do this, since Belgium was a constitutional monarchy, meaning that the king was required to seek formal authorization to act. However, the conniving Leopold's aspirations were foiled only briefly. Determined to gain control of the territory, he devised a plan to bypass the Belgian government by maneuvering fourteen other European countries, acting as a collective body, to grant him permission to function as sovereign over the Congo. In this presumptuous manner, the Congo Free State was established in 1884, with Leopold handed personal ownership of its 15 million inhabitants. "A brand-new state had been created essentially by fiat out of a vast African territory," writes journalist Peter Forbath, "unbeknown to the overwhelming majority of the people who lived there."[6]

To stifle the wave of criticism that followed, Leopold claimed he was taking possession of the Congo expressly to help its luckless inhabitants, his aim being to bring civilization to the Dark Continent. He planned to wipe out slavery, he said, and in other ways improve the quality of life for the entire lot.

The Congo, however, neither wanted nor needed his help, not that it was going to receive it anyway, his altruistic proposal being merely a front. The Congo, an area the size of Western Europe located in the heart of Africa, was a self-sufficient territory comprised of a profusion of societies that had coexisted peacefully for thousands of years. Among other features, its more developed communities possessed their own distinctive arts, religions, monetary systems, judicial procedures, and social customs. Some practiced slavery, too, although those whom they enslaved were usually criminals. Certainly the societies of the Congo did not need civilizing by Leopold's men. Nonetheless, his men arrived, and within a short time created a repugnant state of affairs, one that led a horrified witness, the young writer Joseph Conrad, to compose a haunting story about his observations there—"Heart of Darkness"—a tale that, almost eighty years later, would serve as the model for the film *Apocalypse Now.*

Sir Henry Morton Stanley

The crimes that Conrad and others witnessed in the Congo were committed under the leadership of a renowned explorer, Sir Henry Morton Stanley, a man born illegitimately in Wales and originally named John Rowlands. After leaving his homeland and settling briefly in New Orleans, Stanley fought in the Civil War, then joined the Navy. He next became a globe-trotting reporter, in which capacity he came to the attention of James Bennett Jr., the enterprising publisher of the *New York Herald*. A man with a talent for spotting rousing stories, Bennett subsequently assigned Stanley, in 1871, to perform a task that would change forever the Welshman's life: he asked him track down David Livingstone, the British physician, explorer, and missionary who had vanished three years earlier in the Congo. Moreover, after a strenuous eight-month search, Stanley and his men did indeed find the missing humanitarian, at which time the intrepid explorer supposedly uttered his famous greeting, "Dr. Livingstone, I presume?"

Of course, Stanley enjoyed worldwide acclaim for his brave deed. He garnered still more praise when he began exploring the Congo River in 1874, and, shortly thereafter, trekked across the African continent in a record 999 days. To be sure, his name was fast becoming an illustrious one, with his courageous feats, particularly his rescue of Dr. Livingstone, touching the public's heart and winning its admiration.

Yet there was more to Stanley than this endearing portrait, a more troubling side. He was, in fact, a man who freely bent the truth to fit his own needs, when he did not fabricate it completely. In addition, he was brutal. According to fellow explorer Richard Burton, Stanley "shoots negroes as if they were monkeys."[7] Stanley even wrote in his diary, without sentiment, "We have attacked and destroyed 28 large towns and . . . four score villages."[8] It was no surprise, then, when General William T. Sherman, the man whose troops torched their way across Georgia during the Civil War, seized the opportunity to meet the adventurer when circumstances brought the two men together in Paris. They shared an arrogance and a ruthlessness.

Stanley was not a daring man, however, when it came to sex. By several accounts, he was nearly phobic about sexual contact with women. Perhaps it was for this reason that, as soon as he was old enough, he began spending his time in all-male environments ranging from settlements in the American West to outposts in the jungles of Africa. At one point, he did, as an adult, propose to a seventeen-year-old girl, but he timed his offer so that it occurred immediately before he was to leave the country on a three-year mission, thereby assuring the wedding would never take place. Finally, when Stanley, nearing the age of fifty, did marry, he barely made it to the altar due to nausea and stomach cramps. On his Alpine honeymoon, during which the union does not appear to have been consummated, he was joined by his longtime companion, a man he described as his personal assistant.

"The explorers . . . who carried out the European seizure of Africa," writes journalist Adam Hoschschild, "were often not the bold, bluff, hardy men of legend, but restless, unhappy, driven men, in flight from something in their past or in themselves."[9] In Stanley's case, he may have been fleeing from conventional heterosexual obligations, while, at the same time, seeking the company of men.

Whatever his sexual nature and original reasons for traveling to Africa, in 1878 Stanley returned to the Congo, this time in the employ of King Leopold II, where he was to serve as the territory's administrator. In this capacity, he arrived in the jungle with sixty-nine men in tow and during the next few years erected a small village, cut a fifty-two-mile road, and laid the foundation for a railroad. Soon, however, the materialistic king began demanding that the Congo's wild rubber be harvested, and it was at this time that matters took a particularly lethal turn.

Dancing with the Devil

In the 1890s, Leopold sent droves of officials, supervisors, and soldiers to the Congo to ensure the acquisition of rubber, now a valuable commodity because it could be used in making tires for the newly invented automobile. To impose its harvest, Leopold's men became militaristic, his regime fast becoming one of the most barbaric known to Africa.

Within months of the king's demand for rubber, his administration in Africa devised a forced-labor system in which soldiers seized scores of villages, terrorized their inhabitants, then put them to work. Although their modus operandi varied, his agents were known to sweep into a community, ransack it, and abduct its women. To secure their return, the male villagers would be forced to go into the jungle and collect vast amounts of liquid rubber. Afterward, the women would be returned, but only if the men agreed to purchase them with goats. Following their wives' return, the men were still obliged to harvest rubber for Leopold—in effect, they were his slaves—or their spouses and possibly children would again be kidnapped, but this time maimed or murdered. As for pay, the rubber gatherers usually received none, although in a small number of cases they were accorded a piece of cotton cloth or a brass trinket, a paltry sum by any standard, especially given the intensity of the work itself. In terms of the amount of rubber demanded, a village would be put on a quota system with its output being determined by Leopold's regional representatives. If the quota was not met, its inhabitants would be tortured or worse.

"If the rubber does not reach the full amount required," explained a Danish missionary, "the sentries . . . attack the natives. They kill some and bring the hands to the Commissioner."[10]

More precisely, Leopold's men would sever the hands of adult male victims as proof of their deaths, then smoke them as a preservative measure. Despite the fact that mass murders of this type permanently reduced a village's workforce, baskets brimming with human hands were routinely hauled to Leopold's officials from those regions judged to be unproductive. Such brutal acts were considered object lessons to surviving villagers to continue meeting their quotas.

In other cases, hands were hacked from women and children who were still alive, most often to prod their husbands or fathers to work harder. In one such episode, a missionary reported watching Leopold's soldiers grab a small girl and slice her wrist, the blood soaring four feet from the severed artery. She died within minutes. In another, a boy ordered to harvest rubber was unable to gather the required quantity, so the king's soldiers tied him to a tree and beat his hands with the butts of their rifles. Several weeks later, his hands, crushed and gangrenous, fell off. In still other cases, entire families were traumatized so as to demoralize their members and ensure their submission. "Soldiers made young men kill or rape their own mothers and sisters," reported one villager.[11] Maltreatment was dispensed in work groups as well. "The sentry would find us preparing food to eat while in the forest," said a laborer, "and he would shoot two or three to hurry us along."[12] In village after village, Leopold's men behaved savagely.

As for those inhabitants fortunate enough to escape the bloodbath, they risked death in other ways. They were prone to illness due to malnutrition, fatigue, and the incessant physical and mental abuse of Leopold's agents. In one notable case, a formerly healthy village watched its population plunge from 5,000 to 352 because its residents, weakened and wrecked, had become highly susceptible to sleeping sickness. Under Leopold's "civilizing" reign, death in many guises stalked the Congo.

Meanwhile, the outside world remained unaware of these horrors in the jungles until a few years later, when the truth finally began seeping out. Among the first accounts was an angry letter of protest demanding that the Congolese's human rights be respected, a letter penned by an African-American preacher named George Washington Wilson who had visited the Congo and been enraged by what he had witnessed. He sent his complaint to King Leopold II, with copies to dignitaries in other nations, but its recipients scoffed at the communiqué partly because Wilson was black. Soon afterward, however, a handful of white men from Britain observed and railed against the exploitation and torture of the Congolese, and their fury compelled Leopold to respond. He did so by flatly denying the accuracy of their reports. The British government remained unconvinced, however, so it ordered Roger Casement, who was serving as a consul in the Congo, to take part in an inquiry into the allegations. Casement at that time was a principled statesman who, as a young man, had traveled to the Congo on repeated occasions and worked briefly, albeit indirectly, under Sir Henry Morton Stanley himself.

Roger Casement

Casement was born near Dublin in 1864 to a Protestant father and a Catholic mother, a deeply devout woman who secretly had him baptized in her faith. His parents died when he was thirteen years old, so Casement, his sister, and his brothers were sent to live with relatives in another part of Ireland. Soon, all of his family members came to recognize his distinctiveness.

His cousin Elizabeth, for one, was impressed by the fact he rarely engaged in rough play and never seemed to lose his temper. She also admired his appreciation of the arts and his love of animals. Another female cousin was physically drawn to him, attracted to his cool gray eyes and curly black hair. She found him to have a commanding presence as well, a characteristic that would be noted by others throughout his life.

When he reached the age of eighteen, Casement secured a job as a clerk in a Liverpool shipping company, but soon became bored with the office routine. Two years later, at his own request, the firm made him a purser on a ship bound for Africa, where, upon his arrival, he found his way to the Congo. Naturally, he was fascinated by the territory, so much that he returned again and again over the years, first as a volunteer under Stanley's leadership during which he helped survey the region for a railroad, then as a salaried employee helping oversee its actual construction. Still later, he served as a British representative to the territory.

Throughout his years in Africa, Casement's European peers in the Congo, although competitive and sometimes critical of one another, consistently afforded the Irishman only the highest praise. Even Joseph Conrad, despite his dreadful ordeal in the sweltering jungles, said that making Casement's acquaintance was "a great pleasure under any circumstance."[13] By all accounts, Casement was a man of compassion and integrity.

In terms of his sexual disposition, when he was being hired to oversee the construction of the railroad under Stanley's command, both his personal and professional credentials were scrutinized. Unlike a few of Casement's friends, who wondered privately about his sexuality, Stanley's personnel director appears to have concluded that Casement was heterosexual—or homosexual and discreet, at any rate.

Casement was duly hired and soon praised as an exemplary employee. It came as no surprise, then, when the British government, a few years later, tapped him to establish a consulate in the Congo, then shortly thereafter asked him to participate in an inquiry into the alleged offenses taking place in the region. Casement was familiar with the territory, knew how to navigate its jungles and communicate with its peoples, and enjoyed a reputation for fairness and decency. By everyone's estimation, he was the ideal person for the assignment. What few people knew, however, is that while working under Stanley, Casement had cabled London on several occasions hoping to prompt such an inquiry. Clearly, he was the man for the job.

Casement, now in an official capacity, traveled in 1903 from the capital city of Boma in the heart of the Congo to the region's outlying villages to interview their inhabitants. To this end, he rented a steamer, and with a cook, a helper, and a dog named John, negotiated the treacherous Congo River for the next fourteen weeks. At stops along the way he talked to villagers, missionaries, and Leopold's men in the field, frequently sending irate letters back to London describing the inhumanity he was uncovering. He posted reports to Britain, and without hesitation, voiced his outrage to those in the Congo itself.

Finally, in the winter of 1903, Casement wrapped up his investigation and returned to Ireland to prepare his report, a scathing document, it turns out, that detailed many acts of violence such as those previously mentioned, as well as numerous others. The report noted, for instance, that not only were countless villagers' hands cut off, but their genitals as well, when necessary to prove their sex. It further recounted kidnappings, beatings, rapes, tortures, and mass murders.

When his report was published shortly after its completion, King Leopold tried frantically to discredit it. A follow-up inquiry conducted by the Belgian government, however, confirmed Casement's findings, resulting in the Congo being unceremoniously stripped from Leopold and placed under the Belgian government's control. Casement became a British hero, and King Edward VII announced his plan to award him the prestigious CMG, or Commander of the Order of Saint Michael and Saint George. But Casement, by this time, had begun having doubts about King Edward and British colonialism. It seems his African experiences had sensitized him to the immorality of political oppression. When he returned to Dublin after completing his human rights inquiry, he found himself experiencing the stirrings of Irish nationalism. As with the Congolese whom he had seen ruthlessly oppressed by Leopold's forces, he was becoming convinced that the Irish people were being wrongly subjugated by the English. For this reason, when he was offered the CMG, he graciously agreed to accept it, but not in person. He pleaded illness and stayed in Ireland.

THE AMAZON AND THE PUTUMAYO

The following year, Casement, in need of income, once again agreed to represent the crown when he assumed the post of consul in the Brazilian cities of Para and Santos, then, two years later, accepted a promotion to Consul-General in Rio de Janeiro. It was at this time that his life took a familiar turn. At Britain's request, he arranged to spearhead another human rights investigation, a study of crimes being committed against Amerindians in the Putumayo River region by foreign parties.

The Putumayo, a thousand-mile branch of the Amazon River, meanders through South America where it forms the boundaries of Colombia, Ecuador, and Peru before rejoining the Amazon itself in Brazil. In its territory are oil reserves, lime, marble, and coal, as well as conditions favorable to the cultivation of sugarcane, bananas, corn, and rice. The region also contains rain forests laden with wild rubber trees, and it was the abuse of the native peoples in acquiring liquid rubber that caused Casement to be summoned to investigate. This time, however, the alleged offenses were being committed by a British-owned firm, the Peruvian Amazon Company, and its crimes were believed to be worse than those uncovered in the Congo.

To begin his inquiry, Casement and his associates arrived at the firm's headquarters in La Chorrera, Peru, in September of 1910, and at once set to work meeting with the company's officials. A week later, his team ventured deep into the Putumayo itself, interviewing laborers and examining their bodies for signs of abuse.

From the moment he arrived in South America, Casement also kept a detailed record which became known as one of his *White Diaries*. In it he wrote his thoughts and observations. According to his entries, he was sure from the start that the company's administrators were suspicious of him and wanted him nowhere near their operation. After a few days, moreover, he began sensing that he might be in danger from "this Chamber of Horrors collection of criminals," a fitting phrase given what he had begun learning about their deeds.[14]

He discovered, for instance, that the company would force upon an Amerindian, typically a man, an "advance" in the form of a flannel shirt or a pair of cheap trousers, then require him to harvest rubber for several weeks or months to repay it. In no case was the man given a choice in the matter; he had to agree to the advance and begin work immediately. Thus, the situation was one of forced servitude, accompanied by violence if the laborer did not bring in a sufficient amount of rubber.

Casement found, in this regard, that floggings were common and sometimes so severe that the victims died in the midst of them or shortly afterward. Those who managed to survive carried scars on their arms, legs, and buttocks. In other cases, company men would hoist a worker high into a tree by a chain around his neck, then let go. On impact, the victim would suffer broken bones and, in some cases, a severed tongue. Casement found, too, that natives were placed in stocks for punishment, but a special type built to be extremely tight so as to inflict intense pain and cause injury when locked around the person's limbs and neck. Even more appalling, he discovered a custom-made stock designed for the laborers' children, a device that pulverized youngsters' bones when the company men placed them in the apparatus, then sat on it to lock it in place.

These were not the only tortures he uncovered. Many men were shot to death when they did not deliver enough rubber, while those who were luckier had their testicles beaten with clubs. Some of these laborers also died due to massive hemorrhaging. As for other population groups, Casement learned that company men, in one particularly cruel scenario, had set an elderly woman on fire, and, in another, hacked off a Peruvian boy's head. To be sure, the firm's atrocities were widespread and sadistic, and were being inflicted upon a nonviolent, indigenous people who were entirely blameless.

In terms of provisions, Casement's *White Diaries* describe the Amerindians as "all undersized, some half skeletons . . . with wretched arms and legs."[15] Many, he says, were given only coca leaves to chew for days at a time, the cocaine within the leaves energizing them so they could continue gathering rubber. Throughout his writings, he portrays the laborers as hungry and drugged, traumatized and submissive.

As for Casement himself, the investigation took a heavy toll on him. "I am getting positively ill," he writes at one point. "My nightmare last night was a composite of all these criminals."[16]

At last, after ten weeks in the steamy Amazon Valley, he completed his investigation and left for Ireland. He planned to take a short rest, recover from a minor illness he was enduring, then begin the painstaking task of composing his final report. However, the British government, eager to stop the abuses, asked him to assemble an interim report as quickly as possible. One month later he delivered an abbreviated version of his findings, and the British government sub-

sequently contacted its Peruvian counterpart and demanded that action be taken, which included the arrest of hundreds of the Peruvian
Amazon Company's men in the Putumayo. In addition, the British
government took two additional courses of action.

First, at Casement's urging, it decided not to shut down the company for fear the firm would simply reorganize as a Peruvian business
and continue exploiting the forest people. Instead, it opted to keep the
firm a British enterprise, but to restructure it and monitor it closely
for human rights abuses. Second, to ensure it would remain a benign
company, the government assigned Casement a seat on its board of
directors. As well, it conferred upon him a truly impressive distinction: it knighted him for his "arduous and dangerous service" in the
Putumayo.[17] Thus, Casement's humanitarian efforts led him to the
pinnacle of respectability, a man extolled around the world for his noble character, as well as the recipient of the crown's most distinguished honor; a knighthood was something of a rarity for an Irishman. Despite the adulation, however, he did not rest on his laurels.

THE BLACK DIARIES

Several months later, Sir Roger, as his friends now called him,
traveled back to Peru so he could observe firsthand the operation of
the newly revamped company. Upon arriving, though, he learned that
the firm was being liquidated; unable to use slave labor, it simply
could not stay afloat. Consequently, the statesman, his plans up in the
air, made a decision that would come back to haunt him: rather than
setting sail for Ireland, he chose to stay in the Putumayo for a few
more weeks, a plan that puzzled his friends in Europe since there was
no obvious reason for him to hang about in South America now that
the tainted British company was going out of business. Historians,
however, have proposed a likely reason for his decision to linger in
the tropics, an answer gleaned from his personal journals.

As was customary in certain classes of British society, Casement
kept not only professional accounts of his work, such as his *White
Diaries,* but also private journals in which he recorded his most intimate thoughts, dreams, and deeds. He began keeping a new one during this, his final trip to South America, shortly after he arrived and
learned that the Peruvian Amazon Company was defunct. It appears

that the consul, his services no longer needed in the region, decided to take a vacation and planned to spend it indulging in sex. A meticulous record keeper, he further resolved to keep a chronicle of his erotic adventures, which, it turns out, he had done in the past while living in the Congo and Brazil. These confidential journals came to be known as his *Black Diaries* because they contrasted so noticeably with his renowned *White Diaries.*

Arriving in a Peruvian town, Casement kicked off his new journal by noting that he was about to take a stroll in a local park, and added, "I hope almost at once to come across a good *big* one." Indeed, says biographer Brian Inglis, "for the next fortnight, he pursued good big ones with a dedication that was almost obsessional."[18]

The *Black Diaries* reveal that Casement fancied sex with dark young men, especially those who were well endowed. They reveal, too, that he routinely gave his partners money after sex, then, in his journal, commented on their size and the amount of cash paid to them.

As to the latter, Casement had, for years, fastidiously logged all of the costs he incurred whenever he traveled abroad, so it is not particularly surprising that he would also register the amount of money he paid to his sex partners. It should be noted, too, that commercial sex was commonplace in many parts of South America at that time, so his behavior, in this respect, was not all that unusual. Still, his journal entries, redundant and reductionistic as they were, cause him to appear as a forty-something "size queen" preoccupied with rent-boy sex. A glimpse into his *Black Diaries* reveals such entries as:

> February 28th: *Mario* in Rio . . . Rua do Hospicio, 3$ only fine room. Shut window. Lovely, young—18 & glorious. Biggest since Lisbon July 1904 & as big. Perfectly huge.[19]

> March 2nd: São Paolo. *Antonio.* 10$000 Rua Direita. Dark followed & Hard. . . . Breathed & quick *enormous push.* Loved *mightily. To Hilt Deep.*[20]

> March 12th: Morning in Avenida de Mayo. Splendid erections. Ramón 7$000. *10" at least.*[21]

To Casement's credit, it should be noted that his pursuit of recreational sex does not appear to have interfered with his professional responsibilities. A close reading of his *Black Diaries,* for instance, reveals that at no point during his lengthy Putumayo investigation did he have sex with anyone, South American or European. Rather, the journals speak of his anguish over the plight of the natives or describe the beauty of a moonrise or recount his giving of food to famished villagers. Of the few passages that could remotely be regarded as sexual, they either praise the sensual beauty of the Amerindians, both male and female, or, in rare instances, describe the sexual overtures other men made toward him during the inquiry. In the most forthright of these, a steward aboard a ship that Casement tours makes himself available for sex, with Casement confiding in his diary, "I wanted awfully."[22]

Although he wanted, he did not take. Instead, he abstained from sex until he wrapped up his investigation. As to the reason, we can infer from his journal entries that the Putumayo inquiry was so dispiriting and physically draining that he had little desire for sex much of the time. Then again, when he did want it, he may have been astute enough to realize that being sexually intimate with those he was supposed to be studying could compromise his objectivity. He may also have known that sexual relations, under the circumstances, could be construed as exploitive. Whatever his thinking, the fact is that Casement conducted himself professionally throughout the Putumayo affair, just as he had done during his probe into the Congo offenses. Even so, his *Black Diaries,* in due course, would cause him to be regarded as a thoroughly depraved soul in a scandal that would rock the British Isles.

THE CAMPAIGN FOR IRISH INDEPENDENCE

Upon returning to Dublin, Casement, nearing the age of fifty and physically exhausted, decided to retire. On a full pension from the British government, he intended to spend his remaining years helping the Irish gain a stronger voice in the governing of Ireland itself, a cause close to his heart since his political awakening in the Congo years before.

As with many of his contemporaries, Casement insisted the crown had no legitimate claim to Ireland; an island that, for several centuries, had enjoyed its own language, customs, and identity. The Irish should rule themselves, he argued. He held fast to his opinion throughout his stay in Africa and later South America, where he watched from afar, and avidly supported, the nascent Irish independence movement. He was especially interested in the progress of Sinn Féin, the organization whose name means "Ourselves Alone" and whose aim was to promote cultural and political reform. By the time Casement retired and settled in Dublin, however, he had become disillusioned with the group because it seemed to be making so little headway. For this reason, he took matters into his own hands. In the autumn of 1913, he and a collection of like-minded individuals formed a militant organization called the Irish National Volunteers, a spirited group seeking to return to the Irish people control over their own destiny, first and foremost by breaking from British rule.

To secure moral, political, and financial support for the organization, Casement journeyed to the United States in the summer of 1914, where he received a rousing welcome from the Irish-American communities of Philadelphia and New York City. Although he was heartened by the reception, he was also disturbed by the oppression he discovered, even when it involved tyranny from bygone years. One night, for instance, as he traveled by train, Casement reflected on the plight of the Native Americans, discussing their predicament at length in his diary. He believed, correctly, that they had been badly abused by the white settlers. Furthermore, his distaste over their treatment was not the only aspect of life in the United States that troubled him. Many of his observations dismayed him, causing him to regard the nation as meddlesome and materialistic.

In addition to criticizing American values and behavior, Casement also composed a fiery letter to the editor of a Dublin newspaper, the *Irish Independent,* denouncing the British government and urging that Ireland forge a cooperative alliance with Britain's nemesis of the day, Germany. Upon its publication, Casement instantly became a divisive figure.

World War I had just erupted, it seems, and his letter advised Irishmen not to participate in the conflict even though they were compulsory subjects of the crown. He argued that they had a far more important battle to wage—the campaign for self-governance—and recommended that they devote themselves fully to this task. "No Irishman fit to bear arms in the cause of his country's freedom," he wrote, "can join the allied millions now attacking Germany, in a war that at best concerns Ireland not at all."[23]

Naturally, Casement's opinion inflamed the British government, especially since he chose to express it in so public a manner. Parliament, indignant, thereafter looked upon him as a turncoat and never forgave him. Furthermore, the British government was not alone in its reaction. Many of his supporters in Ireland were baffled by his radical position, a number of whom regarded it as sincere but misguided.

Misguided or not, one thing was certain: Casement felt restless and unfulfilled in the United States yet was wary of returning to the British Isles where his letter had ignited such a furor. So he decided to sail to Germany and planned to seek its backing for the Irish independence movement.

To this end, the former statesman disguised himself so that British undercover agents would not recognize him—he washed his face in buttermilk to lighten his suntanned skin—then boarded a ship for Norway under an assumed name. A young Norwegian sailor accompanied him on the voyage, a gay man he had befriended in New York and hired as an assistant. Their strategy was to travel to Norway, then make a dash for Germany. Their plan was successful; the pair arrived in Berlin in the autumn of 1914 as war thundered around them.

At once, Casement set to work seeking German support for the Irish cause, most notably by soliciting money and weapons for an eventual uprising in which Irish patriots would overpower British forces and take control of their own land. With this objective in mind, he visited German prison camps and met with Irish prisoners of war whose allegiance he sought to shift from England to Ireland. His hope was to enlighten his captive countrymen about the evils of colonialism so they would later unite as a fighting unit and contest British rule. Although, to his knowledge, no plan had yet been made for such an insurrection, from the moment the Irish National Volunteers had been formed it was understood that a rebellion would inevitably occur.

What was not to occur, however, was a fruitful collaboration with the Germans. Despite Casement's best efforts, after several months he concluded that he was wasting his time, that the empire's officials, including Kaiser Wilhelm II, had no real plan to supply him with either cash or arms. For this reason, during the two years he remained there, Casement became deeply antagonistic toward the German authorities, dismissing them as "cads" and "swine." Before long, he also realized that most of the Irish prisoners of war had no intention of joining him, either. Not only did they flatly refuse to turn against their king; they were offended that Casement chose this time and place, as they lingered in foreign prison camps, to challenge their loyalty to the crown. The result is that the former statesman, his hopes dwindling, became so depressed that a friend placed him in a Munich sanatorium where Casement wrote in his journal that he was "sick at heart and soul, with mind and nerves threatening a complete collapse."[24]

His spirits began to lift in the spring of 1916, however, when he learned that freedom fighters in Ireland were at long last planning an insurrection, and that the German government had agreed to send rifles and ammunition to help the some 16,000 members of the Irish National Volunteers in the revolt. His excitement quickly turned to worry, however, when he realized that the shipment itself—20,000 rifles of inferior quality—would be inadequate and the uprising would almost certainly fail. He therefore decided to risk returning to Ireland with the intent to convince the insurgents to postpone their rebellion until they were better equipped, or, at the very least, to lend them a hand if they decided to proceed. "If those poor lads at home are to be in the fire," he wrote in his diary, "then my place is with them."[25]

To this end, Casement sent a letter to the German authorities urgently requesting transportation back to the Emerald Coast. "I will very gladly go to Ireland with the arms," he offered, "and do all I can to sustain and support a movement of resistance."[26] Shortly after receiving their consent, he boarded a submarine that was to escort the ship carrying the rifles, and the two vessels sped under cover of night to the Irish seaboard. Once they arrived, he swam ashore.

"I was happy for the first time (in) over a year," he later told his sister. "I was for one brief spell happy and smiling once more."[27]

Upon setting foot on his native soil, Casement was supposed to have been met by Irish patriots, but instead was confronted by the police, who drove him to Dublin to await transport to London where he would be tried for high treason. Still determined to stop the uprising he believed would be such a profound waste of Irish life, he met that night in his Dublin cell with a Catholic priest and implored him to contact the insurgents. "Tell them I am a prisoner," he said, "and that the rebellion will be a dismal, hopeless failure."[28] The clergyman agreed to convey the message.

The next morning, Casement was taken to London to face his fate, but was calmed by his belief that the insurrection had been halted. Little did he know that the freedom fighters had dismissed the priest's warning, convinced that a suicidal mission was better than no mission at all. Thus, his journey back to Ireland did not lead, as he had hoped, to the end of the rebellion, but rather to the end of his own life.

TREASON AND TRIAL

Arriving in England on Easter Sunday, Casement was held incommunicado in the Tower of London, where he was placed in a vermin-infested cell garbed in the same mud-spattered clothing he was wearing the night of his arrest. Only several days later, at the insistence of friends and lawyers, did the authorities provide him with standard-issue prison attire, and, still later, permit him to talk to others.

As for the revolution, the day after he was incarcerated Irish patriots launched the coup in Dublin, a revolt known as the Easter Rising because it erupted at the height of the religious holidays. In the course of the revolt, freedom fighters occupied government buildings and blew up bridges, and street skirmishes broke out between Irish and English forces for over a week. Over 200 buildings were set afire during this time, the beginning of the Ireland's twentieth-century fight for independence. Finally, the English forced the surrender of the coup's leaders, then promptly shot them. The murder of these men, however, saluted today as the "spiritual fathers of the current Irish Republic," was a profound mistake.[29] Their execution triggered blistering condemnation from Ireland and the United States because they had not been tried in the customary fashion. Rather than being given the opportunity to defend their actions in court, the Crown had dealt with them through martial law, even though the revolt itself was largely over by that point. The prevailing opinion was that the freedom fighters had been subjected to extreme measures not warranted by the situation itself.

Unfortunately for Casement, although he was safe in London, the authorities mistakenly believed he was behind the revolt in Dublin. They suspected he had traveled to Germany where, in concert with German leaders keen on weakening Britain, he had planned the insurrection, then personally escorted the donated weapons back to Ireland for use in the rebellion. Thus, the man who had tried to prevent the uprising was, ironically, the one accused of masterminding it.

The sensational affair stunned the world, having the greatest impact in those nations where Casement had traveled or lived. In Peru, for instance, the reaction was one of astonishment, as well as elation in certain quarters. Those responsible for the Putumayo atrocities, in particular, seized on the situation at once, claiming that Casement's actions proved he was untrustworthy, and, by extension, that the findings of his inquiry were not to be believed. Of course, few bought their desperate argument—the Putumayo findings were airtight—but this did not stop them from trying, in the most transparent fashion, to capitalize on his misfortune.

The reaction in the United States, by comparison, was more sympathetic. The public, it seems, was sensitive to the plight of the Irish people in wanting their homeland to be autonomous once again; the United States, after all, had fought its own war against Britain to gain its independence. Casement was seen as a great humanitarian who had perhaps gone a little crazy as a result of living in the jungle. The major newspapers described him as "paranoid" and having "a screw loose." It was also the consensus that Casement, if found guilty, should not be put to death, that he had done too much good in the world to be killed because of a spasm of excessive patriotism and political naiveté.

Then there was Ireland. As could be expected, the Irish people viewed his actions as sacrificial to the cause of liberty and hailed him as a patriot. Neighboring England, by comparison, regarded him as a traitor. Even in England, however, were those who insisted he should be spared the death sentence if judged guilty, that he should, in fact, receive a pardon in light of his courageous deeds in Africa and South America on behalf of the crown. Foremost in the public mind was the fact that Casement had nearly single handedly saved hundreds of thousands of lives. These and other arguments were voiced in the weeks leading up to his trial in the summer of 1916.

The proceedings themselves lasted two weeks, and, as anticipated, attracted huge crowds and massive media coverage. The prosecution presented its case first, arguing that Casement had organized the Easter Rising and was thus responsible, more than anyone else, for its bloodshed. Adding a degree of brawn to the proceedings, the discourse was delivered by the Attorney General, Sir F. E. Smith.

"The prisoner," Smith declared, "blinded by a hatred to this country, as malignant in quality as it was sudden in origin, has played a
desperate hazard. He has played it and he has lost it. To-day, the for-
feit is claimed."[30]

Casement, he insisted, was not just a malcontent, he was a threat to
the British empire. He had persuaded innumerable Irishmen to challenge Britain's authority, and, worse still, had colluded with its arch-
enemy of the day, Germany. Punishment must therefore be taken, and
it must be decisive. Such was the reproachful flavor of the prosecutor's address, a sermon of fury and indignation. Smith then presented
his evidence, which was circumstantial, and afterward rested his
case.

Next came the defense. Casement had initially wanted to represent
himself in court. He planned to proclaim his innocence in plotting the
Easter Rising, then use the occasion to voice the need for Irish self-
governance and the importance of allegiance to one's own people. "In
Ireland alone in this twentieth century," he intended to say, "is loyalty
held to be a crime."[31] On the advice of legal experts, he reluctantly allowed a promising young attorney named Alexander Sullivan to represent him, a decision he came to regret.

Sullivan originally toyed with the idea of making an insanity plea
using Casement's diaries as evidence. He planned to argue that they
revealed the immense stress he had endured while in the Amazon
Valley. It is true, the journals did make clear the ordeal's strain on
Casement's mental and physical health. After giving the matter further thought, however, he decided an insanity approach would be futile. Casement was not, nor had he ever been, mentally disturbed, and
neither the bench nor the public would believe otherwise. For that
matter, even if he were unhinged the court would probably not admit
it, as Casement was a former statesman and member of the knighthood, the pride of the empire.

In its place, he adopted a defense based on a technicality. According to a rigorous reading of British law, treason occurred when a subject of the Crown "be adherent to the King's enemies in his realm,"
meaning that a citizen conspired with an adversary of the state within
the borders of Britain itself.[32] Sullivan decided to bank on this narrow definition because Casement's deeds had allegedly taken place in
Germany, not Britain, thus the law would not apply. This approach
also carried another advantage: since it consisted of a largely aca-

demic debate about the wording of the legislation, there would be no reason for the prosecution to cross-examine Casement. Indeed, he might not have to speak at all in court; only the attorneys would be involved in the debate. This was a plus, given that a distressing event had occurred shortly after Casement's arrest, one he did not wish to talk about in public.

The police, it seems, while rummaging through his personal effects, came across his *Black Diaries* with their unabashedly homoerotic content. Although the journals were not made public at that time—it would be nearly fifty years before British officials would permit the citizenry to look at them—soon after their discovery all of the parties involved in the trial read them except for Casement's own lawyer, who would not look at them. Such was the grip of the young attorney's homophobia. Thus, the prosecution possessed damaging sexual material it could use to obliterate Casement's character, but Casement's legal representative, by refusing to examine the incriminating journals, could not prepare a defense against it. By pursuing the technicality argument, however, Sullivan believed he was on safe ground. He gambled that the prosecution would not introduce the *Black Diaries* into court since they had no bearing on the subject under discussion. Furthermore, he was right; it did not submit them. Unfortunately, however, the technicality defense itself was so lame that the court readily found Casement guilty. The bench, it turns out, chose to follow the spirit of the law, rather than the letter of the law. It did not matter to the court where the act of treason had taken place, only that it had occurred at all. This was a predictable ruling, one for which a precedent had been set years earlier in a comparable treason trial. In this way, the defense lost the case.

Still, the verdict notwithstanding, it was widely believed that the court would not order an execution. Because Casement had enjoyed a distinguished career as a consul, by now it had become broadly assumed that he would be pardoned, or at most imprisoned, especially after the criticism the crown had received when British authorities summarily shot the leaders of the Easter Rising.

Even Casement himself had come to believe he would not be put to death, mainly because of the impact his execution might have on international relations. The United States, he told friends, had made it known that it did not want to see him hanged. Britain, meanwhile, was eagerly currying favor with the United States, a potential ally against Germany in the war. If the United States opposed his execution, he reasoned, Britain would almost certainly agree to spare his life so as to appease this prospective ally. Although his argument made a certain degree of sense, Casement was, in fact, engaging in wishful thinking. A few weeks later, he came face to face with reality when the British government abruptly stripped him of his knighthood to underscore its outrage. Stunned, he realized the Crown had every intention of executing him, regardless of the American reaction, and thus began bracing himself for death while his supporters launched a campaign to save his life.

Reprieve groups were hurriedly formed to lobby for a pardon. Individual citizens tried to help, too. The poet William Butler Yeats wrote to Britain's prime minister imploring him to reconsider the sentence, while Sir Arthur Conan Doyle, himself a patriotic Irishman, drew up a petition calling for a stay of execution. An impressive document, its signatories ranged from bishops to novelists to physics professors, as well as the presidents of the Royal College of Physicians, the Baptist Union, and the National Free Church.

Essentially, the petition made three arguments for sparing Casement's life. First, it suggested that he may have become mentally unbalanced as a result of his harrowing experiences in the tropics and thus was not responsible for his actions—the insanity plea, once again. Second, it warned that the German government would almost certainly use the hanging, as well as the controversy surrounding it, for propagandistic purposes. Third, it reminded the British government that the United States, at the conclusion of the Civil War, did not execute any of the South's confederate leaders but instead adopted a policy of mercy toward them, a sign of its maturity and compassion as a nation and its desire to heal political wounds.

As for the U.S.' position on Casement's sentence, popular opinion was against the impending execution. The Negro Fellowship League, among other organizations, contacted King George V and requested clemency for Casement, while several influential senators sought President Woodrow Wilson's intercession in the matter. Wilson, however, refused to act because he was not sympathetic to the Irish cause, at least not that of Irish Catholics. Undeterred, the Senate submitted a resolution to Parliament requesting that Casement be allowed to live. Thus, in both Europe and North America, the punishment was opposed.

It was at this pivotal moment that a "pale, narrow-faced, thin-lipped man" named Ernley Blackwell entered the picture.[33] A legal advisor to Britain's Home Office, Blackwell, for reasons unknown, detested Casement and was hell-bent on seeing him hanged. When Blackwell, after the treason trial, happened upon a letter Casement had written while in Germany, one that expressed his plan to return to Ireland to halt the Easter Rising, he evidently suppressed it so the court would stick to its decision and execute the former statesman. Several weeks later the authorities learned about the existence of this letter which more or less cleared the defendant, however, it was disregarded because Blackwell had made them aware of another piece of Casement's handiwork, his *Black Diaries*. Blackwell, it seems, after getting his hands on the journals shortly after Casement was placed in the Tower of London, secretly ordered their homoerotic passages copied. He was certain their exquisitely timed release would assure Casement's execution.

Blackwell thus set about circulating copies of the diaries' gay passages among the gentlemen's clubs of London, and presented them to such personages as the prime minister and King George V. He also arranged for copies to be sent to Washington, DC, and to the American ambassador in London, who was aghast at what he called Casement's "unspeakably filthy character."[34] He even sent them to Casement's old friend, John Harris of the Anti-Slavery Society, who, it was reported, nearly fainted when he read them. A handful of psychiatrists scrutinized the journals as well, and although they did not advise that Casement be locked away in a sanitarium, they did say the journals revealed grave sexual abnormalities.

Unfortunately, the calculated leaking of the *Black Diaries* proved to be extremely effective. The government's ministers discussed the journals among themselves and unanimously agreed that the death sentence was fitting. Likewise, the Court of Criminal Appeals convened, examined the *Black Diaries,* and revisited the treason case itself. After two days of deliberation, it too decided Casement did not deserve a reprieve. That was the end of the discussion. One month later, he was led to the gallows.

The execution was set for August 3, 1916. Following a morning mass, Casement, appearing detached, walked onto the prison yard and stood motionless while his hands were strapped behind his back.

He was then led to the scaffold, where the executioner fastened a noose around the former statesman's neck.

In due course, the command was given, the trapdoor swung open, and Roger Casement, straight and rigid, plunged through it. In this brutal manner, his life was ended.

AFTERMATH: THE FORGERY SCANDAL

The controversy surrounding Casement's death did not die with the man himself. The day after his execution, the British government, finding itself under renewed criticism, felt obliged to release a statement justifying its actions, a statement insisting all over again that Casement had masterminded the insurrection. It further claimed that the court, after his trial, had come to possess important new information proving he was, indeed, behind the revolt. This statement was inaccurate to say the least. The only new material the authorities had acquired was the letter Casement wrote while in Germany, the one Blackwell tried to suppress because it supported Casement's innocence; that, and the *Black Diaries,* which revealed only that he was gay. The government's statement, then, was a fabrication, and not a particularly credible one in that the public basically ignored it.

Meanwhile, Casement's supporters in Ireland and the Irish communities of the United States had begun lionizing him, creating memorials in his honor and composing poems and songs extolling his character and deeds. He was fast becoming a martyr. For this reason, the British government called on one of its favorite propagandists, the poet Alfred Noyes, to counter this mounting significance. Noyes, as requested, set to work undermining Casement's character. Before long, however, his withering remarks backfired. During a visit to the United States a few months after the execution, the poet, rather than quashing the controversy, unwittingly fueled it.

In a newspaper article he wrote while staying in Philadelphia, a city boasting a sizable Irish-American community, Noyes attacked Casement's reputation, saying his sexual deeds were "filthy beyond all description."[35] He added that a pig's trough would be degraded if Casement's diaries were to touch it.

What Noyes did not know is that Casement's sister Nina was visiting Philadelphia and had read his scathing remarks. Furious, she decided to confront him publicly, since Noyes' article had itself appeared in a public medium. To this end, a few nights later when the poet approached the podium in a packed auditorium to give a lecture, Nina jumped to her feet and began denouncing him for insulting her brother's memory. She insisted that she knew her brother well and was confident he was not homosexual. She added that the *Black Diaries,* in her opinion, were most likely forged by the British authorities hoping to turn popular opinion against her brother so he could be hanged without a public outcry. With Nina's accusation, a conspiracy theory was born.

In the years following her public flare-up, proponents of the forgery theory offered several arguments to bolster their claim that the diaries were counterfeit. Four of their assertions, in particular, comprised the backbone of the theory.

First, they pointed out that the man who claimed to have found the *Black Diaries,* Basil Thomson, the chief of Scotland Yard's Criminal Investigation Department, may well have lied, especially since he gave four different accounts of their discovery. Moreover, Thomson was himself later arrested in a London park and convicted of sexual misdeeds with a prostitute, a verdict that was upheld on appeal. His reputation as a public official, then, was anything but sterling, with his history suggesting he could be receptive to corruption, especially if ordered to engage in shady actions by his superiors. Proponents of the forgery theory further noted that Thomson, after discovering the diaries—or, more precisely, after claiming to have discovered them— was knighted, with skeptics viewing this as a reward for his dubious actions.

Second, they pointed out that the British authorities had a clear motive for fabricating the journals. After the trial, public opinion was opposed to Casement's execution, especially in Ireland and the United States. By concocting damaging sexual material, however, the officials knew the public would be less resistant to the idea of the hanging, that there would be much less commotion about it. It is true that the British government knowingly used the *Black Diaries,* whatever their actual origins, to turn the tide of public opinion against Casement in order to bring about his death. In so doing, the government discredited itself.

Third, proponents of the forgery theory argued that Casement's enemies in the Putumayo region would surely have known about, and capitalized on, his distinctive sexual tastes. They said his foes, among other measures, would have confiscated, then exposed, the *Black Diaries* that he carried in his baggage during his travels. Casement's adversaries in South America, however, as well as those in the Congo, were genuinely surprised by the revelation of his same-sex liaisons, with this being construed as additional proof that the diaries were a sham.

Fourth, Casement's family and most of his acquaintances had little reason to think he might be gay. Although he did not date women, people who knew him well assumed he was more interested in human affairs than love affairs. They also insisted he showed no "signs" of homosexuality. In this regard, Casement's friend John Quinn, an influential Irish-American attorney, declared that neither in tone of voice nor in Casement's outward behavior was there anything degenerate about him. Of course, this was a telling statement about society's limited understanding, and jaundiced view, of gay sexuality at that time.

Still, despite the points made in support of the forgery argument, the evidence supporting the diaries' authenticity was even more compelling. According to historian Benjamin Reid, who researched Casement's life, "nowhere in all the evidence is there any real sign of his being romantically or passionately drawn to a woman." Instead, "they were quite simply friends and allies, comrades, good fellows; he seems never to have thought of them as sexual creatures."[36] Ernest Hambloch, Casement's vice consul in Rio de Janeiro, adds that it was common knowledge in diplomatic circles that Casement fancied young Brazilian men.[37] This was known several years before the journals were leaked.

Furthermore, Casement had long written poems confirming his love of men; verse that he kept largely to himself and that was made public only after his death. Curiously, no one, including those nearest to him in life, questioned his authorship of these poems.

Supporting the authenticity claim, too, were the journal entries themselves, which described homoerotic interludes that occurred in remote outposts such as Africa and South America and in cities such as London and Dublin. As well, the sexual passages were interspersed with an even larger number of entries that were nonsexual, all of which were written in chronological order dating back over a decade.

Those who believed the journals were authentic also noted that Michael Collins read them soon after their discovery and was convinced they were the genuine article. Collins, a high ranking Sinn Féin official, president of the Irish Republican Brotherhood, commander-in-chief of the Irish National Army, and an eventual signatory of the 1921 treaty making Ireland a republic, had known and admired Casement for years. He was also familiar with his style of thought, as well as his handwriting, and recognized the journals as a Casement product.

Finally, there is no clear record that Casement himself ever denied writing them. As a matter of fact, one of his worries in prison was that the journals would be made public and he would be called upon to discuss them in court.

The most cogent evidence, then, indicates that the *Black Diaries* were written by Casement. Even so, a sizable segment of the population refused to believe it. In the years following his execution, the forgery argument thrived, with those both for and against it holding fast to their positions. Gradually, however, the controversy began to pale until 1936, when two poems by Yeats and a popular biography about Casement were released in Britain, works asserting that the *Black Diaries* were counterfeit. Within weeks, the issue took on renewed power, then subsided again until 1954 when another biography and an influential article returned public attention to it. Politicians and historians, at that time, hoping to finally put an end to the conjecture, petitioned the British government to permit the citizenry, especially handwriting experts, to examine the diaries. The authorities, however, balked at the notion, their refusal only fueling the suspicion that the journals were the work of government forgers. At last, after five more years of pressure, the government opened the diaries to public inspection, with historians examining them and pronouncing them genuine. But even this did not put the matter to rest. A year later, in 1960, yet another article asserting the diaries were fake caught the public eye and fired up the debate for a new generation. In this fashion, the controversy persisted, in fits and starts, for nine decades. If nothing else, the story has been a boon to journalists.

As recently as 2000, yet another historian, Angus Mitchell, proposed an inventive argument suggesting that the journals were doctored. His claim prompted the prime minister of Ireland, Mr. Bertie Ahern, to call for new forensic analyses of the incriminating diaries, as well as a symposium on the subject. Although the conference took place, it was arguably of little value given that it was structured in such a way as to exclude from discussion the whole subject of Casement's sexuality, a queer omission to say the least.

Alluding to Roger Casement in a recent speech, Ahern said that under legislation enacted in 1993, homosexuality is no longer a crime. However, he said this as he was seeking renewed studies to determine whether the diaries were counterfeit. Ahern claimed that England, the source of the professed forgery, still had in its possession Casement materials that it was refusing to make public. Thus, despite his outwardly progressive stance toward homosexuality, Ahern's actions suggest, as with many Irish citizens, he may still feel the need to find Casement "not gay," the equivalent to a verdict of "not guilty" of homosexuality.

Fortunately for Ireland, there are within its borders those men and women who are themselves gay or bisexual and who are more appreciative of diversity. Among them is activist Jeffrey Dudgeon, who has himself written a book about Casement. In a refreshingly candid statement, Dudgeon recently told London's *Sunday Times* that Casement "showed himself to be an early exemplar of what is now commonplace in the male gay community."[38] It is hoped that Dudgeon's realistic perspective will itself become commonplace in Ireland someday. At this stage, however, many in that nation steadfastly refuse to accept the fact that Casement, a renowned nationalist who died for the principle of Irish independence, was also a lover of men.

MORAL, SOCIAL, AND POLITICAL DYNAMICS

The Casement affair tells us much about homophobia and the nature of scandal. For one thing, it illustrates the doggedness and the destructiveness of an ancient Judeo-Christian teaching, namely, that a homosexual act is the result of a moral lapse, a surrender to some dark, depraved urge, and that gay people are therefore morally corrupt. It was because of this belief that many of Casement's contemporaries came to regard his behavior as paradoxical. Because he performed deeds of remarkable courage and compassion in the Congo and the Amazon Valley, he was considered a man of impeccable character, yet when rumors of his homosexuality began to emerge, these new reports baffled his admirers who believed same-sex relations were decadent. How could a distinguished humanitarian and self-sacrificing patriot be, at the same time, a gay man and an adventurous one at that? Casement was all of these things, however. To his way of thinking, he was behaving in a consistently moral fashion whether he was protecting natives in faraway lands, seeking foreign aid to ensure Ireland's liberty, or sharing his love with another man. Ireland's more traditional elements, however, unable to reconcile these seeming discrepancies in his character, did not stop to question their assumptions about the moral dimensions of same-sex love but instead concocted a means of preserving their longstanding beliefs by lopping off a basic aspect of his personality, his sexual orientation. This is how the forgery argument came to be, and part of the reason it still exists today. By eliminating Casement's gayness from the equation by insisting the *Black Diaries* were forged, traditionalists have been able to maintain a one-dimensional notion of morality, one that allows only heterosexuals to be the freedom fighters, the humanitarians, the national heroes.

The Casement affair also demonstrates the problems that arise when the public intrudes into an individual's private life. By several accounts the British people, most notably the government and media, became inordinately interested in Casement's after-hours conduct. Like the American obsession with former President Clinton's trysts while in office, the British became fixated on Casement's intimate liaisons. This signaled a rupture of the crucial distinction between the public and private realms.

Casement, the citizenry seemed to forget, was entitled to a personal life, including a sex life. He had been a consul, not a pope, such that his erotic encounters were, in the words of historian A. L. Rowse, "his own private affair, no one else's business. . . . [O]nly his public activities were proper matter for public comment."[39]

To many, however, the sexual gossip *was* considered relevant. The *Black Diaries* garnered public notice because their entries exposed the unorthodox nature of Casement's sexual tastes, with this presumably revealing something about his character, something sinister. Although homosexuality was certainly not unknown in Britain at the time—there were men and women at all levels of society rumored to be gay—Casement's passions were rather exotic. As we noted earlier, he paid dark, well-endowed young men for sex, most often intercourse in which he was the receptive partner, and this violated at least five British rules of acceptable sexual conduct. Not only did Casement's encounters involve prostitution with those of the same gender who were several years younger than he, they also crossed racial lines and consisted of an act regarded by many as demeaning for a man: he adopted the "womanly" role during intercourse. Although his alleged political activities in Germany violated British treason laws, his sexual activities defied Britain's long-held definitions of manhood. Collectively, his deeds were believed to reveal his lack of respect for, and disloyalty to, British values, principles, and ways of life. In this way, the fusion of public and private culminated in his death.

The scandal demonstrates, too, the ways in which a political faction may deliberately keep alive a controversy, no matter how old or irrelevant it might be, in order to reap its benefits. By repeatedly dredging up the accusation that the English forged the *Black Diaries* so as to hang an Irishman, England's critics in Ireland have been able to exploit the controversy for propagandistic purposes for nearly a century now. Just as the English capitalized on Casement's intimate diaries to secure his execution, the Irish have made abundant use of the resultant forgery charge to pummel the English. Without a doubt, there are political blocs that have a vested interest in ensuring that the dispute continues since, for them, it is a weapon they can use against their opponents.

Last of all, the incident reveals the power of scandal. Sadly, Casement's political deeds in Germany and especially the mêlée over his sex life eclipsed his rather astonishing achievements as a consul. This was a man who saved hundreds of thousands of lives in the Congo and the Amazon Valley. More than any one person, he brought to an end the torture and exploitation of countless men, women, and children on two continents. Outside of the British Isles, his name is largely unknown; a dismal epitaph for such an extraordinary figure, and one that illustrates the manner in which a scandal may obscure the good in a person while showcasing merely the provocative.

At the present time, Irish leaders continue to claim that the British government is in possession of crucial information about the genesis of the *Black Diaries,* information it keeps under lock and key, shrouded in secrecy. This claim is rejected in London. Certainly there is no compelling reason for English officials to squirrel away antiquated documents and to refuse, nearly a century after the fact, to hand them over to their Irish counterparts. Such allegations appear to serve little purpose at this juncture.

Thanks to modern technology, today there exists a far more definitive means of settling the dispute about the *Black Diaries'* origins, which is exemplified by a rigorous study conducted recently at the Giles Document Laboratory in London. A state-of-the-art investigation overseen by a council of forensic scientists from Ireland, England, and Scotland, the Giles research is considered the most objective ever to have been performed on the diaries. Among other procedures, it consisted of an evaluation of pollen residue on the journals' pages, microscopic analyses of the handwriting, electrostatic deposition analysis of the indentations, and ultraviolet studies of the ink. In March 2002, the results were announced and the findings confirm that the dairies were, in fact, the work of Roger Casement. Yet even in the face of these high-tech and largely incontestable methods, a handful of opponents materialized within hours of the information release to cast doubt on the findings in a desperate attempt to keep alive the remote possibility that Casement might have been heterosexual. Fortunately, such naysayers presently comprise a small minority, which appears to be dwindling and may eventually disappear altogether. The fact is, the body of evidence attesting to the *Black Diaries'* authenticity, especially with the recent addition of the Giles findings, is now so substantial that a critical mass may soon be reached, one that will prompt the Irish people, at long last, to lay to rest the controversy over Casement's sexual orientation and accept him for what he was: a man whose sexual and emotional experiences with other men were so meaningful that he kept a written account of them, a humanitarian who risked his life to stop the exploitation of those who could not fend for themselves, and a patriot who died struggling to restore his nation's sovereignty.

Chapter 2

A Question of Conspiracy:
The Murder of Pier Paolo Pasolini

In a daring coup d'etat staged in 1922, Benito Mussolini became Italy's prime minister. Three years later, he strong-armed his way to dictator, a position he held for the next two decades. During this time, Il Duce, as he was commonly known—a nickname meaning "The Leader"—was a force to be reckoned with, routinely launching deportation drives and terror campaigns to intimidate and control the Italian people.

As for the reasons behind his coerciveness, Mussolini and his organization, the ultraright National Fascist Party, believed it was the state's responsibility to meet the needs of the citizenry, and that this duty could best be discharged if the state exercised total control over fundamental components of society, particularly labor and industry. Il Duce and his party further believed the citizenry should submit to their authority.

"Everything within the state, Nothing outside the state, Nothing against the state," was the Fascists' slogan, and by all accounts they took this catchphrase to heart.[1] Among other deeds, they set up tribunals to confront those they regarded as morally, socially, or politically incorrect, which oftentimes resulted in imprisonment of scores of gay citizens, members of the Mafia, and, of course, antifascists. They also micro-managed key aspects of national life, deciding, for instance, what Italy's factories could manufacture, what the presses could print, and what the schools could teach. They even decided what movies the public could watch, going so far as to take action against films that, in their opinion, failed to promote Mussolini's agenda of fervent nationalism and traditional family values. This included banning or "cleaning up" through the editing process American films that happened to play in Italy during the 1920s and 1930s. This task, it turns out, was no small feat, since roughly 80 percent of the motion

pictures screened in Italy during that period were produced in the
United States, and were either subtitled or dubbed for foreign audiences.[2]

Films that were outlawed or altered by Mussolini's regime included such classics as *A Farewell to Arms, Lost Horizon, Robin
Hood, Mutiny on the Bounty, The House of Rothschild,* and the Marx
Brothers' *A Night at the Opera.*[3] The Fascists also prevented Italian
audiences from viewing the film *Dead End* because it contained
scenes of juvenile delinquency, and *Wings Over Honolulu* because it
showed a divorced couple, a pairing that flew in the face of Mussolini's stance against marital dissolution. Even *Romeo and Juliet,* the
quintessential love story, was banned. "The double suicide bothered
censors," explains James Hay, professor of film studies at the University of Illinois.[4] To be sure, Mussolini's minions, like the priggish
village censor in Giuseppe Tornatore's 1989 masterwork *Cinema
Paradiso,* were quick to put the scissors to any picture expressing
views that strayed from Il Duce's own professed moral beliefs and
political ideals.

Even after Mussolini was assassinated in 1945, political factions in
Italy continued using their leverage to condemn motion pictures, particularly those perceived as critical of whatever faction happened to
wield power at the moment. An example of this oppressive mentality
can be found in the case of gay filmmaker Pier Paolo Pasolini. Born in
1922, the year Il Duce seized power, Pasolini was subjected to attack
by unscrupulous political forces throughout his career. There are
even those who claim, with some justification, that malevolent political blocs devised his death in 1975 in a dark, lonely soccer field on
the outskirts of Rome. This brutal murder forever silenced a leading
intellectual voice considered by many to be a troublesome one. To
understand the cultural significance of Pasolini, including his controversial death, it will serve us well to revisit his upbringing during the
Fascist era, since it is in his childhood and adolescent years that one
finds the conditions that helped set the trajectory of his remarkable, if
scandalous, life.

PIER PAOLO PASOLINI

Pier Paolo Pasolini was born in the northern Italian city of Bolo-
gna. His family later moved to the rustic village of Casara. Carlo, his

father, was a staunch Fascist of minor nobility, a man known for his relentless authoritarianism. Pasolini's mother, Susanna, was a gentle yet spirited antifascist from an impoverished provincial family. As could be expected, given such fundamental differences, the Pasolinis' marriage was a combustible one, with young Pier all too often finding himself torn between his parents' personalities, principles, and politics. It was not only in his home that he experienced discord, however. He also faced it at church, in school, and in the everyday happenings of his neighborhood. In Italy during the Fascist period, conflict besieged the people at every turn, and this included the children.

As to the reasons behind all this strife, Italy, during the 1920s, was recovering from World War I and was in a state of flux. Suffering from what has been described as a national inferiority complex, it was in dire need of stability and direction. The citizenry, however, rather than confronting unpleasant truths about their nation, the first step toward maturation and progress, placed their faith in the overblown promises of Mussolini, believing, naively, that he could help Italy regain its footing through his simplistic, hard-line measures. Not everyone agreed with Il Duce's approach, however, and it was for this reason the nation was in turmoil throughout his reign.

Of course, Pasolini, as a youngster, knew little about the Fascist Party. He simply endured the consequences of its policies. He did know, however, that his father was one of its loyal members, as well as the man he feared most in the world. So intimidated was he by his father, in fact, that he sought comfort from his mother, a devoted schoolteacher who, among other deeds, instilled in him a love of poetry. His attachment to verse became unshakable. At the age of seven, Pasolini, to his mother's delight and his father's chagrin, began writing poetry, and soon came to appreciate the essay, the short story, and the novel.

During his adolescence, Pasolini continued nurturing his fascination with the literary arts while also developing a passion for the visual arts. As he gained experience as a writer, he became convinced that freedom was essential to the creative process; that restrictions, personal or political, stifle self-expression and should thus be removed to the greatest extent possible. In time, this insight would prompt him to reject the theory and practice of Fascism, and, along with it, his authoritarian father.

In this regard, Pasolini learned to use literature to extract himself from his father's world of suffocating morality, and attached himself to his mother's world of culture and the arts, according to longtime friend Enzo Siciliano. In a state of rebellion, Siciliano said, Pasolini began using poetry "as a vehicle to express against (his father), and against every face of authority, the truth of being 'different.' "[5]

Certainly one way in which young Pasolini was different became evident during his teenage years and involved his attraction to other boys, a trait that alienated his father. Although the elder Pasolini "loved the fact" that his son was performing well in school, says Siciliano, he "could hardly love . . . his homosexuality."[6]

Pasolini, as well as his parents, was aware that he was gay, but he kept this fact from his friends throughout his adolescence. As a result, his companions assumed he was heterosexual, despite the fact that some of them enjoyed mutual masturbation with him from time to time, a not uncommon pastime among youths in the provinces.

One person who did know about Pasolini's homosexuality was a boy with whom he had sex on a regular basis, a friend who was altogether comfortable with their erotic dalliances. This youth's healthy attitude was in contrast to that of Pasolini, who, while sexually active, continued having reservations about same-sex relations. Even so, Pasolini was not as upset by his homosexuality as was an older woman who happened upon the two youths while they were "in the act" and threatened to turn them over to the police. This incident terrified Pasolini, causing him, for several years thereafter, to associate shame with same-sex desire and to live with a morbid fear of being caught and punished. In due course, his fear would become a reality.

Controversy in Cordovado

The year was 1949 and Pasolini was twenty-seven years old. By this time in his life, he had written poetry for several years and self-published his first book of verse, *Poeisie a Casara*. Although prominent critics praised the collection, hailing it as a notable artistic achievement, a portion of the reading public thought it was self-indulgent and was taken aback by its homoerotic allusions. Regardless, the book was a minor success.

In addition to publishing his poetry, Pasolini also taught school for many years, tutored countless students, and wrote several notable essays, which garnered him respect as a poet, teacher, and intellectual as well. He had become politically active along the way, too, joining the Communist Party and accepting a political appointment in his town. It was in this manner that he had become a prominent, influential man in his province. Because of his visibility and especially his political position, he had also become a target of the Christian Democratic Party, the Communist Party's principal opposition. This antagonistic state of affairs helped bring about, or at least intensify, his first scandal, one that would serve as the prototype for many more to come.

A local priest who was a member of the Christian Democratic Party warned Pasolini through an intermediary to cease his work on behalf of the Communist Party or risk forfeiting his career as a teacher. Pasolini ignored the threat and persisted in his political work. He also continued writing, teaching, and pursuing recreational sex.

As for the latter, he had been sexually active with other males for many years by this time. Although he was still at odds over this aspect of his life, he had nevertheless disclosed to several close friends that he was gay. This was because forthrightness, by now, had become vitally important to him, whether it involved his sexual disposition or his political convictions. This candor would eventually become one of his greatest assets and one of his great liabilities.

In terms of the scandal itself, it happened one autumn evening when Pasolini and his cousin Nico attended a religious celebration, the Festival of Saint Sabina, in the village of Cordovado, near Casara. During the festivities, Pasolini met four boys, all in their mid-teens, whom he persuaded to have sex with him. Nico was also invited to join, but declined. So without further ado, Pasolini vanished into the fields with the boys, emerging sometime later and exclaiming to his cousin that the experience had been "unforgettable."[7]

As it turns out, the four youths, while later quarreling among themselves about the incident, were overheard by a bystander who reported the matter to the police. At once, the authorities questioned them.

"Pasolini began to kiss (a young man)," concluded the official report, "putting his tongue in his mouth and massaging his member and then, taking down his trousers, exposed his own member."[8] Pasolini then brought himself to orgasm, paying the youth a hundred lire afterward. The report added that the other young men watched the encounter, and one or more may have participated. The police subsequently arrested Pasolini for attempting to corrupt minors and engaging in obscene acts in public.

Devastated and suicidal, Pasolini reluctantly attended his trial shortly thereafter, during which he was acquitted of the corruption charge but found guilty of the public obscenity allegation. Two years later, however, during the appeal proceedings, all charges were dropped due to a lack of evidence, but by this time the damage had been done.

The fact is, the Christian Democratic Party drew on the sordid episode to diminish Pasolini's credibility in the public eye. Although there was no doubt that he had engaged in sex with underage partners, thus violating society's moral standards, not to mention the law itself, his political enemies used his offense to their advantage. After his conviction, Pasolini was fired from his job as a schoolteacher, and was barred from tutoring students in private. The Communist Party also expelled him on the grounds that those who were gay or lesbian were not true communists since their sexual behavior reeked of bourgeois degeneracy. Even the residents of the region shunned him for having taken liberties with their sons. In this way, Pasolini lost his most cherished affiliations, as well as the public influence he had acquired over the years. Yet despite being traumatized, he failed to grasp why his improper conduct with the juveniles had provoked such an uproar, later confiding in a friend that he felt no regret about having had sex with the boys. Thereafter, he viewed himself as a sexual outlaw, an identity he defiantly embraced for the rest of his life.

Life in Rome

In the aftermath of the scandal, Pasolini found himself in his late twenties, jobless, and very much at sea. Certainly he was no longer welcome in the town of Casara, and the imbroglio had further divided his parents, bringing enormous turmoil into their home. For these reasons, one snowy winter morning he bundled up his mother Susanna and together they made their way to the railway station. There, they used borrowed money to catch the early train to Rome. They did not tell Pasolini's father they were leaving, nor did they say goodbye to the townspeople. They simply took their leave, and for the most part never looked back.

Arriving in Rome, they sought out a relative who helped find a small apartment for Pasolini, a flat in a ghetto on the outskirts of the city. A job was also secured for Susanna as a live-in maid for an architect. Literally overnight, the circumstances of Pasolini and his mother had changed dramatically.

As could be expected, times were tough in the beginning, with Pasolini accepting virtually any writing assignment that came his way. At first he worked as a journalist for a noncommunist governmental newspaper, then as a proofreader and book reviewer. He also wrote pieces for national radio and continued publishing poetry. Soon he turned his hand to novels. His fiction, predictably, became an amalgam of Catholicism, communism, and eroticism.

In terms of Catholicism, since childhood Pasolini was deeply moved by its themes and imagery, and would remain so throughout his life. He believed the religion preserved the agrarian tradition and thus helped meet the needs of the people. He thought the same of communism, an ideology that continued to speak to him through its concern for the poor and dispossessed. In fact, Pasolini became even more devoted to this ideology as a result of the scandal in Cordovado. He believed his persecution as a gay man, as he chose to view it, allowed him to experience oppression firsthand, thereby enlightening and liberating him. Years later, one of his friends would suggest that Pasolini's tendency to see himself as a wizened martyr also may have been influenced by his Christian roots, specifically "by the idea that the more one is rejected, the more he is the vehicle and receptacle of truth."[9] Certainly, it does appear that Pasolini believed he gained insight into the human condition because of his suffering, in spite of the fact that his troubles were largely of his own making.

As for the eroticism that infused his texts, it became even more pronounced after he fled to Rome. No doubt this was because he had become entranced by the sexual ambience of the city and particularly by the youthful urchins who peopled his neighborhood, underprivileged young men who sold themselves on the street. Soon, these same youths would begin making their way into the pages of his books.

Before long, Rome's indulgent young men would also make their way into Pasolini's bed. Indeed, it seems he embarked on an erotic romp once he hit the city, picking up young men in the cinemas, the bathhouses, and the rest rooms along the Tiber. He and gay poet Sandro Penna even arranged a contest between themselves to discover who could seduce the most boys within a given time frame. He enjoyed procuring sex from teenage hustlers too, even going so far as to write to his cousin Nico in Casara beseeching him to sell the Pasolini family's beloved collection of Greek and Roman classics and send him the proceeds so he could buy more sex. Pasolini, an avowed communist with a professed concern for the impoverished and alienated, did not consider his sexual encounters with the young prostitutes to be a means of exploiting the lower class, but rather morally neutral transactions serving to fulfill his sexual needs and his partners' economic ones. To be sure, he was seeking sex with a vengeance, while placing the scandal in Cordovado far behind him. As a self-proclaimed sexual desperado, he was simply doing what he yearned to do, regardless of the repercussions.

This is not to imply, however, that Pasolini spent his days and nights exclusively on sexual binges. Even as he reveled in passion, he continued writing, and from 1951 to 1953 was permitted to teach once again. Providentially, he was then offered the chance to write a film script. The upshot was that he would earn enough money to move himself and his mother into an elegant apartment in an upscale neighborhood. His father, Carlo, moved in with them shortly thereafter. For the next eight years, Pasolini forged a remarkable career, writing screenplays for such filmmakers as Federico Fellini and penning scores of poems, novels, essays, and translations, all the while holding fast to his communist convictions. Although one of his novels created such a stir that he wound up in court defending himself against a pornography charge, he was nevertheless coming to be regarded, at a national level, as a truly gifted man. Finally, in 1961, he found himself in the position to make his first motion picture.

Scandal on the Screen

As it turns out, Pasolini's career in the cinema would prove to be even more controversial than his writing career because his films would reach a much larger audience, an enhanced visibility causing him to be held to a higher standard of social responsibility. But his cinematic efforts were also more provocative.

His first film, for instance, *Accatone* ("The Scrounger"), tells the story of a devious pimp/thief who lives in poverty in a Roman shantytown and forces his live-in lover, a naive and pitiful woman, to prostitute herself. When she discovers that Accatone is secretly carrying on with other women, she reports his illegal activities to the police, who place him under surveillance and nearly nab him when he tries to steal a truck. He succeeds in giving them the slip, however, only to accidentally crash his getaway vehicle, which kills him. Pasolini said the film depicts the plight of the impoverished.

Accatone premiered for critics at the 1961 Venice International Film Festival and created quite a commotion. Right-wing figures, most notably members of the Christian Democratic Party, attacked the picture's sexual decadence, violence, and fatalism, while left-wingers, namely those in the Communist Party, criticized its portrayal of the disenfranchised as sleazy, selfish, and spiteful. The government subsequently sought to ban the film, arguing that it was unsuitable for viewing, particularly by those under the age of eighteen, but a trial conducted a few months later concluded that it was permissible entertainment. Even so, when it premiered before the general public shortly thereafter, right-wing extremists—young neofascists—overran the theater and assaulted members of the audience, ripped seats from their foundations, and hurled ink at the screen.

Pasolini responded to his critics by arguing that Italian audiences did not wish to acknowledge the poverty that lurked on the outskirts of their cities, and that they were refusing to face the fact that conditions had not changed appreciably since Mussolini relinquished power, which the Christian Democratic Party acquired. He sidestepped the concerns of the Communists, however, who felt the film betrayed the very people it was meant to help. Writes Naomi Greene, author of *Pier Paolo Pasolini: Cinema As Heresy,* the filmmaker "first raised the hopes of those who wanted a socially conscious cinema but then quickly disappointed them."[10]

Unrepentant, Pasolini released his next film, *Mamma Roma,* the following year. It starred Anna Magnani as an aging streetwalker who, displeased with her life, resolves to remake herself. When conditions force her to return to prostitution, however, her son, who is a young adult, becomes so distraught that he turns to thievery. Soon finding himself behind bars, he dies, strapped to a wooden table, while his grieving, guilt-ridden mother tries to jump out a window.

Mamma Roma opened at the 1962 Venice International Film Festival and was immediately declared obscene because it contained the words "shit" and "piss."[11] This judgment, however, an obvious case of harassment, was reversed within a month. Nevertheless, efforts to interfere with the film persisted. Several days later, when the movie premiered before the general public, neofascists were again on hand to assail Pasolini and his cast members as they arrived for the screening. This time, however, the filmmaker was primed for the occasion, throwing the first punch before the entire crowd was hauled off to police headquarters.

In the ensuing months, Pasolini and the actors associated with him increasingly found themselves the targets of verbal and physical attacks on the streets of Rome. By all accounts, the situation was heating up.

It was into this crucible that Pasolini released *La ricotta,* featuring Orson Welles, a film centering on the Crucifixion and culminating in an indictment of modern society's degradation of the Christian religion. To no one's surprise, *La ricotta* was declared blasphemous when it opened, even though it actually supported the Christian faith, and Pasolini was ordered to stand trial. What is surprising is that he was found guilty and sentenced to four months in prison, although he was quickly granted amnesty. Still, the case proceeded to ignite a national debate about film censorship and the role of the artist in society. Furthermore, such a discussion was sorely needed at this time, since the campaign to legally suppress *La ricotta* had been put into motion by uncompromising religious leaders who did not take kindly to its message.

To clarify his views of religion and, at the same time, appease the authorities—authorities he regarded as dolts—Pasolini next released *The Gospel According to Matthew,* whose premier the neofascists, rather predictably by now, tried to disrupt. Nevertheless, the film was embraced by critics and public alike, delighting the Christian Democrats and the Catholic Church and not unduly annoying the nation's communist or socialist factions. Almost immediately, however, Pasolini returned to making films plainly intended to provoke all manner of outrage. Among them was *Teorema,* one of his most acclaimed and controversial motion pictures, an inventive blend of politics and religion that would inflame diverse segments of Italian society.

Teorema

Filmed in 1968, *Teorema* is the story of an affluent household in Milan composed of a mother, father, son, daughter, and maid. Into this home comes an attractive but ethereal young man, a stranger, who sexually seduces each person by appealing to their unseen desires and dreams. Gradually, through their affinity with him, the family members and their servant find themselves liberated from their insipid lives and placed on the path to personal transformation, until, that is, the stranger unexpectedly departs, leaving them midway through their odysseys. The tragic result is that each person, with the exception of the maid, disintegrates in what has been referred to as a "serial self-destruction."[12]

Teorema is Italian for "theorem," and Pasolini used this mathematical term to refer to the mechanical process revealed in the story. Once the stranger enters the family's life, his appearance in their home but a random event, a human equation is brought into existence that must be played out according to fixed rules, such as those comprising a mathematical law, an inevitability. Writes Millicent Marcus in her book *Italian Film in the Light of Neorealism,*

> The plot of *Teorema* is completely arbitrary and unmotivated, depending upon a mechanism external to the narration to keep in it motion, as Pasolini's title, taken from the discipline of mathematics, immediately suggests. The plot is thus manipulated by an abstract logic, the logic of the theorem, which imposes its own rigid, alien structure on the events of the storyline.[13]

"The entire film," she adds, "works on this pattern of mathematical precision."[14]

Teorema is also a metaphysical piece. Indeed, "Teorema" is the name of a renowned medieval theological tract. In this regard, film critics have suggested that the stranger is actually a Christ figure who brings to the meaningless lives of the family members the promise of spiritual regeneration. His premature departure triggers their degeneration because they have surrendered their former selves to him before fully attaining the replacement, their "higher" selves. Since their conversions are incomplete—they have not yet reached the Promised Land—they can only disintegrate.

On a more worldly level, *Teorema* was a political statement, a scathing commentary on the bourgeois experience of the 1960s. This was an era when Italy was wracked by discord among its political factions and social classes, perhaps best illustrated by the growing number of riots erupting in the streets. Particularly loathed was the upper middle class, which is the element depicted in *Teorema,* and one that Pasolini himself detested. Among other complaints, he believed the well-to-do were spiritually defunct, saying in an interview that "the bourgeois has lost the sense of the sacred."[15] It is for this reason that the working class maid in *Teorema* is the only member of the household to fulfill the spiritual journey. Enlightenment is accessible to her because she comes from humble circumstances and presumably is closer to God.

Finally, *Teorema* can be viewed as a portrait of Pasolini himself. After the scandal in Cordovado and his escape to Rome, he seemed uncertain and unsettled, a condition that persisted throughout his life. Over the years, he also became increasingly masochistic, all too often placing himself in circumstances guaranteed to undermine his best interests. This extended to his sex life. Friends later recounted how they often had to rescue him from sexual encounters gone awry while filming in the Middle East, Africa, and Europe. Surely it was no accident that the names of the male characters in *Teorema* are very similar to those of Pasolini himself, and that these men, deeply tormented, ultimately come to a bad end. The film may be therefore viewed as a mathematical demonstration, a religious parable, an indictment of the bourgeoisie, and as a close-up of Pasolini himself, most notably his confusion, despair, and self-destructiveness.

As for *Teorema's* reception, upon the film's release the pope declared it a disgrace and the Italian government banned it for obscenity. Censors were piqued because its male lead, handsome twenty-nine-year-old actor Terence Stamp, was shown briefly in the nude. They also were annoyed because the movie took a swipe at the bourgeoisie, and dared to use sex—male homosexuality, no less—as a metaphor for religious experience. One critic even misunderstood the film as implying that those who are gay or lesbian tend to prey on upright, unsuspecting families. In such ways, *Teorema,* whether interpreted correctly or incorrectly, came to be regarded, in the late 1960s, as the filmmaker's most contentious creation.

The early 1970s would prove to be a sunnier time for Pasolini. His "Trilogy of Life" series was brought to the screen; motion pictures shot in exotic locales and served up with wit, spectacle, and male frontal nudity. Drawn from classical literature, they consisted of *The Decameron, Arabian Nights,* and *Canterbury Tales,* and although some viewers considered them pornographic and others found them plodding, they were generally well regarded by the critics and the public. In fact, these were the films that brought Pasolini international fame. Undermining their success, however, was a letter published by the filmmaker himself shortly after their release, a document repudiating them. It seems Pasolini decided to distance himself from what he considered their naïveté, arguing that it was impossible to make endearing movies about historical eras because modern-day capitalism had sullied the present and the past as well. Personalizing the matter, he added, "Private sexual lives (like mine) have been subjected to the trauma of false tolerance and/or corporeal degradation: what constituted joy and sorrow in sexual fantasies has turned into suicidal disillusionment and amorphous ennui."[16]

The fact is that Pasolini, when he renounced his trilogy in the 1970s, had begun showing signs of deterioration, a corrosive process that eventually affected diverse aspects of his life. As for what triggered this downward spiral, no single factor seems to have been at work; rather, several events appear to have impinged upon a man known to have difficulty coping even under the best of circumstances. One of these events, judging from Siciliano's account of the filmmaker, was the departure of actor and lover Giovanni "Ninetto" Davoli.[17]

Pasolini first met Davoli while filming *The Gospel of Saint Matthew* in 1964. The filmmaker was forty-one years old at the time. Davoli was fifteen. Pasolini was instantly smitten with the young man, a peasant by birth whose family had moved to a shantytown on the edge of Rome. Physically striking and emotionally radiant, Davoli had curly dark hair, bright, dancing eyes, and a childlike, comic manner. He exuded freshness and life, along with a sense of wholesomeness, and thus complemented Pasolini's darker, more troubled personality. The filmmaker subsequently cast Davoli in *Saint Matthew,* as well as in successive films, including leading roles in the "Trilogy of Life" series. The older man also took the younger one into his heart, the two remaining intimate until Davoli reached his late teens, when, by law, he was obliged to report for military service. It was during the ensuing months, while he was in the army, that Davoli came to realize he desired women; a discovery that crushed Pasolini, who believed he had lost, for all time, his companion. In reality, Davoli would marry and have children, but would nevertheless remain Pasolini's loyal, if platonic, friend to the end. The filmmaker was not yet aware of the strength of Davoli's allegiance, however, and so felt cast off and behaved accordingly.

After Davoli's heterosexual awakening, Pasolini became deeply depressed, composing poems marked by a sense of loss and anguish. He also pursued a more self-destructive sex life, seeking out anonymous partners who, his friends say, left him "injured and bleeding."[18] To be sure, Pasolini, a man who fellow filmmaker Roberto Rossellini once described as "very tormented," was now more disturbed than ever.[19] Eventually, he did meet a bashful, dark-haired young man from a rural province—shades of Davoli—whom he invited into his life and his country home, an isolated medieval tower.

It was in this remote edifice that the filmmaker hired a photographer to snap pictures through a window late one night, photos of Pasolini himself as he lounged naked in his home. He explained that he was planning to use the prints to illustrate a novel he was writing. It was also during this period that he began production on his final motion picture, *Salò: The 120 Days of Sodom,* a work designed to be both shocking and offensive and considered by many critics to be his worst film, although a small number defended it as an inspired tour de force.

Salò: The 120 Days of Sodom

A blend of Mussolini's Fascism and the Marquis de Sade's lurid tale of sadomasochism of the same title *(The 120 Days of Sodom),* the film is a study of power and victimhood. Set in the Republic of Salò, the region of northern Italy that Hitler returned to Mussolini in 1944 after Nazi troops sprang Il Duce from prison, it was a time and place in which Pasolini himself had lived. It was, he said, "an epoch of sheer cruelty, searches, executions, deserted villages, all totally useless."[20]

In the film, four sexually frustrated but powerful libertines—a noble, a priest, a banker, and a judge—order their underlings to kidnap eight young men and eight young women and herd them into an enormous, yet bleak, villa. There, they subject the captives to ritualistic sexual torture, ranging from flogging to castration, with the film culminating in the victims' wholesale slaughter while the libertines watch and pleasure themselves.

Critical reaction to the film was razor sharp. "Fascism is obscene, and that was to be Pasolini's point," said a reviewer for *The Washington Post,* "but turning it into campy idiocy proves only the impotence of the filmmaker's esthetics."[21] *Salò,* said another, "is an unfortunate attempt to reinject eroticism into genocide."[22] Still another intoned, "*Salò* is the kind of swan song you'd prefer to see even your worst enemy spared."[23] Then there was Rex Reed of the *New York Daily News,* who called the film "a despicable and nauseating piece of garbage that would disgust the denizens of a 42nd Street grind house."[24]

As could be predicted, given its deliberately repellent subject matter, the picture, for several years, was banned in virtually all nations, and attempts have been made in recent times to outlaw it again. Even in the weeks immediately following its completion in 1975, the Italian people were not allowed to see it, although accounts of its gory content became widespread during and shortly after its filming, gossip that did nothing to counter Pasolini's reputation as a man in decline.

Pasolini's political statements most certainly did nothing to improve his image. By late 1975, he had managed to alienate practically all of the country's religious and political factions. The Catholic Church had long abhorred him, as had the Christian Democratic Party. But now the Communist Party, whose policies and actions he criticized, regarded him as a major embarrassment as well. The Communists considered him a fraud and a nuisance, a man who claimed to care for the poor yet drove flashy cars, lived in opulent quarters, sported designer clothing, and preyed on needy slum kids for sex. Even so, some of the Party's younger members did have a modicum of respect for the filmmaker, particularly those who, like Pasolini himself, disagreed with the Party's strategies. A larger share of the nation's youth, however, were not at all fond of him by now.

University students, for instance, most of them liberals, were both perplexed and angered because Pasolini, a man who had long promoted himself as a friend of the masses, refused to support their movement for a fairer, more representative government. He further infuriated Italy's liberal element by taking a stand against the legalization of divorce, as well as abortion. Although he had mocked the family in *Teorema* and had referred to marriage as "a funeral rite," the filmmaker now claimed he had always revered the tradition of heterosexual marriage and the family. Also irritating was the fact that Pasolini, although homosexual, kept a noticeable distance from Italy's budding gay and lesbian community, even going so far as to oppose its efforts to secure gay rights legislation. His antigay stance did not prevent him from cruising for underage sex partners six nights a week at precisely the same hour each evening; indeed, his sexual addiction was in full swing until the moment of his death.

The unavoidable truth is that the filmmaker appeared to be adopting political positions based on their ability to attract attention and provoke rage rather than on their ideological merits. It is for this reason that his numerous political diatribes, taken as a whole, seemed so contradictory during this, the last year of his life. In the same way that his sexual encounters resulted in his own bloodshed, and just as *Salò* had revolted censors to such an extent they banned the film internationally, Pasolini's pronouncements on contemporary affairs appeared perfectly calibrated to incite the wrath of nearly all sectors of society. To be sure, he was a disturbed man pushing society's tolerance to the limit, not unlike the ill-fated characters in his films. Certainly this was evident in his final public declaration in October 1975, a hysterical, rambling attack published shortly before he was killed.

In a scathing newspaper piece, Pasolini declared that the Italian ruling class should be put on trial for

> unworthiness . . . misappropriation of public funds, price-fixing for oil companies . . . collaboration with the CIA . . . responsibility for (neofascist) terrorism . . . anthropological degradation, the disgraceful condition of schools, hospitals and every other basic public institution . . . the wildcat explosion of popular culture and of mass media, and the criminal stupidity of television.[25]

It came as little surprise when Pasolini turned up dead a week later. The public was taken aback, though, by the viciousness of the crime itself.

MURDER IN OSTIA

Early on November 2, 1975, a Sunday morning, Ninetto Davoli was awakened by a phone call. It was Graziella, a Pasolini cousin temporarily living with the filmmaker and his mother in their palatial house in Rome. She was worried because, several hours earlier, the police had stopped by to inform her that a youth had been arrested behind the wheel of Pasolini's silver Alfa Romeo. The young man, it seems, had stolen the car. Even more ominous, when Graziella sought to tell Pasolini about the matter, she discovered he was not in the house. It is for this reason that she phoned Davoli. He was the last person known to have been with the filmmaker, the two having dined together at the Pommidoro Restaurant earlier that evening, along with Davoli's wife and two young sons.

Alarmed by the disappearance, Davoli hurried to the police station and offered his help, and his assistance was accepted at once. It seems a bulletin had just come into police headquarters: a corpse had been discovered in the seaside town of Ostia, southwest of Rome. Suspecting it might be the filmmaker's body, the authorities asked Davoli to accompany them to the scene to identify the body. What they came upon was truly grisly.

The corpse was lying face up in the dirt. Nearby were two pieces of wood splattered with brain tissue. The face was mutilated, both ears sliced, and one ear dangled from the head. The throat was cut, the torso mangled, the chest distended and misshapen, and the hands scraped and raw. Bizarrely, a bloody shirt sat on the ground a few yards away, creased neatly with the buttons fastened and the sleeves folded in back, laundry style. Davoli confirmed that the body was indeed that of Pasolini.

Meanwhile, at police headquarters, authorities continued questioning the seventeen-year-old caught with the Alfa Romeo. His name was Giuseppe Pelosi, but friends called him "Joey the Frog."[26] A well-known prostitute, Pelosi had a history of arrests and had been sentenced on three different occasions to juvenile prison for, among other crimes, auto theft. He had been out of jail only two months at the time of the murder.

During the interrogation, Pelosi denied stealing the car, instead offering several far-fetched excuses for having been caught with it. He did ask, however, that the police return three items he had left in the vehicle: a pack of Marlboros, a cigarette lighter, and a ring with a red stone and bearing the inscription "United States." Only later would investigators ponder the significance of this request. Finally, after four more hours of his denials, officials told Pelosi that they had found Pasolini's body in Ostia, and it was then that the hustler admitted he may have killed the filmmaker but insisted it was in self-defense.

In Pelosi's version of events, at ten o'clock Saturday night he was standing next to a kiosk in a Roman train station when Pasolini— "a faggot," in the youth's parlance—parked his car and walked over to him.[27] According to the youth, Pasolini offered him a gift if he would get in the car, and Pelosi agreed. A few minutes later, they drove to a café where Pelosi ate spaghetti (Pasolini ate nothing), after which the filmmaker suggested they go to a secluded soccer field and have sex. He offered to pay the young man $25 for his services. Pelosi agreed, so they left the city.

At the playing field in Ostia, Pasolini turned off the car, bent over Pelosi, and performed oral sex on him for a few moments, but did not bring him to orgasm. Instead, he allegedly told the hustler to get out of the car and walk onto the darkened field. Pelosi did as he was asked. Pasolini followed him a few yards and then, still standing behind him, began caressing Pelosi's buttocks. Pasolini then asked Pelosi to take off his jeans, but the youth balked at the request. To encourage him, or perhaps to tease him, the filmmaker supposedly picked up a wooden stake from a broken picket fence and put it against the back of the young man's pants. Pelosi, suspecting Pasolini may be planning to rape him, spun around and faced the older man.

"You're crazy," he said to Pasolini, then walked quickly toward the car.[28] Because he could not see clearly in the gloom, Pelosi stumbled and fell, and Pasolini seized the opportunity to jump on top of him and strike him in the head with the stake. Pelosi managed to fling the stake into the distance, then he scrambled to his feet and dashed toward the car. Pasolini, determined to stop him, caught up to him and began beating him again.

Pelosi then spotted a wooden plank, which he broke over Pasolini's head. He also kicked him "in the balls" a couple of times.[29] Pasolini, oblivious to the blows, continued pounding Pelosi in the face until he could barely see. Finally, the young man, in a panic, pummeled Pasolini with the plank until the filmmaker, wheezing, crumpled to the ground. Hurling the splintered board into the darkness, Pelosi raced to the car and drove off into the night. He said that he may have run over Pasolini while fleeing the soccer field, but could not remember for certain. Down the road a few minutes later, he pulled over to a fountain to rinse off the blood. After that, he jumped back in the Alfa Romeo and sped down the highway until he noticed that the police were in pursuit. He tried desperately to outrun them but soon realized he could not, so he stopped the car and attempted to elude them on foot. Moments later, the authorities captured him and took him into custody.

Later that day, in spite of the hustler's confession, the authorities decided to perform an exhaustive investigation of the murder. They were well aware that suspects confess for all sorts of reasons, and that not all declarations of guilt are true or at least comprehensive. Besides, it was no secret that Pasolini had many enemies, some of them potentially deadly. A painstaking inquiry was launched, one that, within hours, began yielding several unexpected findings.

For starters, investigators learned that Pasolini had been receiving anonymous death threats during the week leading up to the murder. They also were unable to locate Pelosi's cigarettes and lighter in the car where he had left them, although they did find a cheap green sweater; a garment that fit neither Pasolini nor Pelosi, which had not been in the vehicle when Graziella cleaned its interior a few hours before the murder. Disturbing, too, was the fact that several pairs of footprints were discovered near Pasolini's body, footprints that were not those of soccer players. Investigators were surprised to find the filmmaker's blood on the passenger door and the roof of the car, since Pelosi had said their altercation took place several yards away from the vehicle. Experts also determined that neither the wooden stake nor the plank found at the site—the plank was rotten—was substantial enough to have produced the wounds on Pasolini's head and body. He was clubbed with a heavier, more lethal object, one that investigators could not find at the scene.

As for Pelosi, when the police apprehended him, his clothes were neat, clean, and virtually blood free, and his body was unscathed. Except for a small cut above his eyebrow that occurred when he slammed on the brakes during the police chase, he was entirely unharmed, unlike Pasolini, who had been reduced to pulp in tattered, blood-drenched clothing.

The initial findings pointed to the collusion of several individuals in the slaying. Investigators surmised that Pelosi may not have murdered Pasolini, but merely lured him to the soccer field, then, after the assault, drove the Alfa Romeo as one of the getaway cars. One of the real assailants, perhaps the one wearing the green sweater, may have slid into the passenger seat of Pasolini's car by placing a bloodied hand on the door to open it and the other on the roof to steady himself.

Later, this same assailant may have taken Pelosi's cigarettes and lighter while getting out of the car. Pelosi took the blame for the homicide, because he knew that if he did not, the same fate that had befallen Pasolini might well await him.

In the ensuing weeks, the investigation continued to produce unsettling findings. Among other conclusions, an autopsy revealed that the kick to, or possibly the bludgeoning of, Pasolini's testicles had produced a massive internal hemorrhage. Wrote one official who reviewed the coroner's report, this blow, in all probability, was "dealt by one person while others held the victim to receive the *coup de grâce*."[30] Then there was the matter of the body's location. The corpse was not lying in the path of the car. The automobile had been deliberately steered to run over Pasolini. Not only that, it then backed up and crushed him again; impacts that caused his heart to explode. Finally, eyewitness accounts provided a different version of events at the train station than the one given by Pelosi.

At the depot in Rome, for instance, it was discovered that Pasolini did not get out of his car and, by chance, walk over to Pelosi, who was standing beside a kiosk. Instead, the filmmaker remained in his vehicle, the doors locked and the windows rolled up, while a gang of hustlers retrieved Pelosi and took him to Pasolini. Thus, the two may have known each other, their tryst prearranged. Support for this notion comes from the staff at the Pommidoro Restaurant, who recalled that Pasolini, after finishing his meal with the Davolis earlier that evening, hurriedly asked for the bill. "Otherwise, I'll be late," he said, a comment suggesting he had an appointment elsewhere.[31]

Furthermore, later that same night, after Pasolini took Pelosi to a café for spaghetti, the hustler convinced the filmmaker to drive him back to the train station where the young man talked briefly to the other prostitutes. It is not known what they discussed. Afterward, he and Pasolini left for Ostia, although it is not certain that this remote destination, twenty miles outside of Rome, was the filmmaker's idea. Instead, Pelosi may have suggested the out-of-the-way site at the behest of others.

Adding to the mystery, a newspaper reporter in Rome received an unsigned letter sometime after the murder. On the night of the slaying, it said, several hustlers at the train station had witnessed another car carrying four men that was following Pasolini's Alfa Romeo.

These men—presumably the real killers—were recognized by the prostitutes, one of whom apparently wrote the letter.

"We knew those four very well," it said. "They threatened to kill [Pelosi] if he said a single word about it."[32]

Such troubling issues notwithstanding, Pelosi stood trial a few months later with the government prosecutor portraying him as the killer. A principal piece of evidence was the ring, the one with the red stone and the "United States" inscription Pelosi had left in the car. Investigators found it not in the Alfa Romeo, but on the ground by the corpse, a finding the prosecutor presented as inconvertible proof that Pelosi was indeed the executioner. To many experts, however, this "clue" seemed a bit too tidy, too perfect to be credible. They proposed that Pelosi had been a patsy, a pawn stage managed by professional assassins to take the heat for a murder. The real killers planted the ring beside the body so as to frame the youth and ensure their own freedom.

If this was their scheme, however, it was only partially successful. After reviewing the evidence and deliberating for several hours, the court found Pelosi "guilty of the crime of voluntary homicide," but added, "in company with others not known."[33] Pelosi, technically a juvenile, was then sentenced to nearly eleven years in prison.

A few months later, though, when his case came up for appeal, the court found itself in an untenable position. It had sentenced the youth to a prison term for murder, yet, in the same breath, declared that he had not acted alone. For that matter, the court had been unable to determine Pelosi's actual role in the killing, having admitted it did not know what had happened the night of the murder or precisely who, or even how many people, had been involved. The court thus revised its earlier ruling to state that Pelosi had, in fact, been the sole killer, thus justifying his prison sentence.

Despite the court's calculated change of opinion, the public remained convinced the macabre murder was the product of multiple killers. The evidence left little room to believe otherwise. The Italian people, including Pasolini's colleagues in the film industry, Bernardo Bertolucci among them, did not hesitate to voice their suspicions. To be sure, after the homicide the public had a heyday trying to identify the culprits in what became a national whodunit.

Conspiracy Theories

Of course, there were, from the start, those who believed Pasolini invited his own death, this being the "suicide by proxy" school of thought.[34] He was certainly known to have been fascinated with sadism and masochism, *Salò* a case in point. He was also known for being drawn, rather compulsively, to rough trade. So taking these facts into consideration, many observers, among them some of Pasolini's acquaintances, surmised that he may have knowingly arranged a sex session with an unstable and potentially violent rent boy whom he collected at the train station and drove to an isolated location. The filmmaker chose this remote site, it was posited, because it helped ensure the hustler would feel defenseless and alone. In this regard, those familiar with *Salò* noted that Pasolini had said in an interview that he placed the film's sexual tortures in a remote villa because only there, in such an isolated setting, would the victims realize there was no chance of being rescued, thus intensifying their horror and despair.

Next, proponents of this theory suggested that Pasolini, at the deserted playing field, aroused the hustler with oral sex, then intentionally provoked him by trying to foist intercourse on him, even physically prodding him with a piece of wood. The youth, vulnerable and afraid, responded savagely, as Pasolini had anticipated. Although this scenario addressed most aspects of the crime, it contained a crucial flaw: it failed to take into account the presence of more than one killer, the blood in the car, and the other evidence collected at the scene, shortcomings that led to a more plausible variation on the same theme.

In the alternative version, proponents proposed that a gang of hustlers sexually tortured Pasolini, thus accounting for his battered scrotum, then killed him. This premise was not all that unreasonable considering that three weeks before the murder, Pasolini had, in fact, been dragged from his car in downtown Rome and beaten with chains by several male prostitutes. He never told anyone why the hustlers had assaulted him, and his friends found it odd that the filmmaker, although injured in the ordeal, refused to report the attack to the police. One thing was evident, however: Pasolini had somehow managed to acquire formidable enemies in the sex trade, just as he had amassed them everywhere else by that point.

It is also rather telling that a few days after the trial began, a young male prostitute from the train station arrived to testify at the proceedings, and, as he walked past Pelosi, said to him, "Decide to tell the truth. . . . You were not alone."[35] This witness then testified that Pasolini had been massacred by four hustlers whom the filmmaker, in the past, had entrapped at Ostia, apparently one at a time, and tried to force into intercourse. When they had refused, struggles ensued, with Pasolini driving off, stranding each of them at the faraway spot. Later, these hustlers compared notes, identified Pasolini as the perpetrator, and plotted their revenge. Unfortunately, the court did not pursue this rendering of the homicide because the witness inexplicably retracted his testimony a week later.

Still another theory, a political one, concerned the Christian Democratic Party, an organization that was unmoved by the filmmaker's demise, taking the position that Italy had lost not an artist and a polemicist but a sexual predator and a provocateur. Of course, the party had every reason to dislike Pasolini. Throughout his life, he had quarreled with the Christian Democrats' efforts to govern the nation, being particularly derogatory in the diatribes he had published shortly before his death. For that matter, he was slated to denounce them, yet again, at a rally in Florence the week he was killed. But while the Christian Democrats had a reason for wishing to see the filmmaker put out of commission, there was no evidence tying them to the murder. Nevertheless, rumors persisted.

Then there was the "neofascist" hypothesis. The neofascists had always hated Pasolini, this being the faction that had disrupted his film premiers in years past. As the extreme right of Italy's political spectrum, the neofascist bloc was worried because the more moderate right-wing Christian Democratic Party was striving to reach a compromise with the left-wing Communist Party. As it stood, the two parties had long been at odds, but had begun forging an agreement whereby the latter would have a stronger voice in the government. The neofascists opposed this pending conciliation, however, fearing that the Christian Democrats, by cooperating with the Communists, would shift the nation to the left. As for Pasolini, because the neofascists regarded him as a prominent left-wing figure, they were suspected of orchestrating his murder as a way of signaling their disagreement with the approaching compromise. To this end, the theory goes, they had capitalized on his reputation as a sex addict with a penchant for rent boys by staging his death in such a way as to validate his unsavory image. In so doing, they had, by design, concocted a scene straight from a Pasolini film.

Adding credence to this hypothesis, at least in the public mind, was a statement Pasolini made shortly before his murder. In an interview, when asked if he was surprised that right-wing extremists had not attempted to silence him, he replied, "I'm amazed they haven't tried it, once and for all."[36] After his slaughter in Ostia, many believed the neofascists had, at long last, done just that.

Even this was not the end of explanations. In the months following the assassination, still more conspiracy theories emerged, including one that sought to hold the Communist Party responsible for the murder. Its premise, which enjoyed a certain plausibility, was that the Communists wanted Pasolini removed from the scene because he had begun publicly accusing them of inertia and ineffectiveness. More to the point, he seemed to be trying to drive a wedge between the organization's younger and older constituencies.

There were also those theories charging the Mafia and the Catholic Church with the slaying, as well as one proposing that Pasolini was executed because of the film *Salò,* despite the fact that the picture had not yet been released. The nation's various political elements got into the blame game too and accused one another of the crime in an effort to win the allegiance of the Italian people, not a surprising turn of events given this tempestuous period in the nation's history. Furthermore, such musings continued well beyond the 1970s. Even today the controversy persists, with innovative works intermittently released, most notably an acclaimed 1995 documentary that reexamined the circumstances of the slaying and speculated on the identities of the assassins.

In the final analysis, Pasolini's death proved to be as sensational as his life, a state of affairs that would have delighted him to no end. By all accounts, this was a man who made a notable contribution to Italy's political conversation and to its arts—his poetry, prose, and films occupy a unique place in twentieth century Italian culture—while, at the same time, exploiting scores of young men. These deeds, or misdeeds, were not accidental. The truth is, Pasolini thrived on conflict. It was his lifeblood. Throughout his years, he studiously positioned himself for controversy, enthusiastically courting, embracing, and perpetuating discord.

Three days before his death, he defended this propensity in a Paris interview, and his words speak volumes.

"I believe to give scandal is a duty, to be scandalized is a pleasure, and to refuse to be scandalized is moralism," he said.[37]

If this statement reflected his true feelings about the social and political import of controversy, then Pasolini had certainly performed a public service, albeit a dubious one, in that he had managed to wear the cloak of scandal not only to the grave, but beyond it.

Chapter 3

An Accusation of Obscenity: Radclyffe Hall and *The Well of Loneliness*

"I would rather give a healthy boy or a healthy girl a vial of prussic acid than this novel," declared James Douglas in a scathing editorial published in London's *Sunday Express.* "Poison kills the body, but moral poison kills the soul."[1]

The critic's five-column broadside ran under the headline, "A Book That Must Be Suppressed," and, indeed, this is what he set out to accomplish. The date was August 19, 1928, and Douglas, besides being a journalist and newspaper editor, was the author of such books as *The Unpardonable Sin* and *The Man in the Pulpit.* He was also an influential figure in conservative political circles and a well-known grandstander. As for the target of his diatribe, it was the novel *The Well of Loneliness,* a nonerotic, mannered book calling for understanding and tolerance of love between women. Due to Douglas's blistering review, however, the work came to be regarded overnight as both scandalous and dangerous. Worse still, it became the subject of arguably the most biased obscenity trial in the history of Great Britain. For numerous gay and straight writers across the nation, it became a cause célèbre, a legal and artistic melee galvanizing their support for literary freedom. No one fought harder for the book to be published, however, nor was anyone subjected to such a trouncing than its author, Radclyffe Hall, herself a fervent Catholic and a member in good standing of Britain's social elite.

PORTRAIT OF THE ARTIST

Radclyffe Hall was born in 1880 to an unstable, self-centered woman named Mary Jane Diehl Hall. After failing to abort the pregnancy, Mary Jane, throughout her daughter's childhood and adolescence, made it clear to Radclyffe that she had been unplanned and unwanted and was still unwelcome in the family. The mother clearly disliked her daughter and did not hesitate to dip into the child's inheritance to further her own social ambitions. "Radclyffe owed nothing to this brainless and egotistical mother," says Vera Brittain, a writer of that period.[2] To be sure, Radclyffe openly detested her mother, as did many others who knew the woman.

As for her father, Radclyffe Radclyffe-Hall—or "Rat," as he was more commonly known—he was a well-heeled cad who was in bed with the family maid when his daughter was born. Educated at Eton and Oxford but seldom gainfully employed, he abandoned his wife and daughter three weeks after the birth. Even so, Rat, although hopeless as a parent, did manage to provide his child with a considerable fortune. It seems he was the only son of Dr. Charles Radclyffe-Hall, a prominent physician and tuberculosis specialist, who was also the president of the British Medical Association, the founder of a sanitarium, and the author of two medical books. From this relative, Radclyffe inherited a sizable sum of money, an amount so substantial it placed her in the enviable position of not having to work (or marry) for financial security. She was thus able to live her life as she saw fit, and she began by calling herself John.

The reason for the name change was simple. A product of the times in certain respects, John believed she possessed so-called male qualities, among them assertiveness, an aptitude for business, and an attraction to women. She also felt at home in men's clothing. As a young adult, she developed a liking for trousers and jackets, and, as she grew older, a monocle and hat. She loved tobacco, too, especially green cigars, nicotine being her only vice, and a minor one at that. At the age of seventeen, John began enjoying what proper Brits considered a truly unspeakable vice: she immersed herself in back-to-back love affairs with other women, relationships she found emotionally and sexually gratifying. For this reason, she came to be regarded as something of a libertine by many of her more straitlaced peers. Due to her family pedigree and personal wealth, however, John continued to be accepted by society provided she played by its rules, meaning that she agreed to maintain a degree of privacy and decorum in her same-sex romances.

Perhaps the most consequential of these relationships occurred when she was twenty-seven, a deeply loving and multifaceted attachment that, among other benefits, helped steer her toward a career as a novelist. It started in the summer of 1906. To attend a women's tennis championship, she traveled to the provincial town of Homburg, England, and took a suite at the Hotel Savoy. There she met a comely fifty-one-year-old socialite named Mabel Veronica Batten, better known as Ladye, who was on holiday with her aging husband George, the former secretary to the viceroy of India. A sophisticated but curious couple, Mr. and Mrs. Batten, while affectionate and respectful of each other, kept separate bedrooms on separate floors. John soon discovered why, for it was at the Savoy that Ladye, drawn to the younger woman's attractiveness and self-confidence, set out to become intimate with her. As it turned out, this did not take long.

"I was wax in her hands," John recalled, "but those hands were entirely trustworthy. She was to become a spur to my work and from the first my unfailing inspiration."[3] Whereas before the affair John had toyed with the idea of a literary career, she had not pursued it in any dedicated, consistent fashion. As a child and young adult she had written verse, and some of her poems were published and a few were even set to music. Over the years, she had also penned several short stories. Never had she attempted to write a book, however, nor had she seriously considered the prospect. Instead, it was Ladye who encouraged her to do so, even going so far as to introduce her to a prominent London publisher. Still, John was not ready to make such a commitment. Several more years would pass before she decided to take on the challenge of the novel.

When at last she did, however, it happened rather suddenly. In 1921, although still enamored with Ladye, John was living with her new lover Una Troubridge, who was to remain by her side for the rest of her life. As John recalled it, she and Una were staying at a small guest cottage where they witnessed the disturbing spectacle of an elderly lady browbeating her adult daughter, treating her as a servant, and draining from the woman her very essence. John, appalled by the scene, one that may well have stirred memories of her own wretched relationship with her mother, resolved to write a novel about unappreciated daughters. The result was *The Unlit Lamp,* which she published two years later and dedicated to Ladye.

Ensnared by the creative process, John continued writing. Her next novel was *The Saturday Life,* followed by *Adam's Breed,* the story of a dejected waiter who starves himself to death in search of God's mercy. Rather unexpectedly, given its doleful theme, the latter book was remarkably successful. Published in 1927, it sold nearly 30,000 copies during its first three weeks, establishing John as a commercially viable author. It was at this time, her reputation secure, that she decided to write an honest, sympathetic account of the lesbian experience.

In Britain during the 1920s, lesbians finally seemed to be gaining recognition and respect, at least in upper-class society. It was during this decade, for instance, that John and Una became fixtures on the London social scene, developing friendships with such luminaries as Noel Coward and rubbing shoulders with Colette, Somerset Maugham, and Virginia Woolf. Yet despite such social progress, enlightened literary works about lesbian love remained nonexistent, a deficiency John felt singularly qualified to remedy. More than that, she considered it her duty. For this reason, in 1927, she ensconced herself at the Hotel Pont Royal in Paris and threw herself wholeheartedly into a book about gay love, a 500-page tome she wrote in longhand because she had never learned to use a typewriter. The result was *The Well of Loneliness,* her groundbreaking book.

THE WELL OF LONELINESS

The novel tells the story of a troubled yet indomitable woman of conscience named Stephen Gordon, born in a picturesque English village to prosperous, devoted parents. The Gordons, it seems, had originally hoped for a son they could name in honor of the father's favorite saint, but are delighted nonetheless when their child turns out to be a girl. Even so, they proceed as planned and christen her Stephen. Kind, generous, and full of understanding, they subsequently provide her with a wholesome, privileged childhood.

Yet as Stephen grows older, she gradually comes to realize that, in some respects, she is different from other young women in the village. When Martin, a local man, proposes to her, for instance, she at once becomes distraught and balks at the offer. Surprised by the intensity of her response, she later asks her father why she reacted so viscerally, but he does not answer. It seems he already suspects his daughter is a lesbian; he simply does not know how to explain it to her. Sympathetic and concerned, he delays talking to her about the matter until, inauspiciously, he is crushed by a falling tree. The up-shot is that Stephen must discover her sexual nature for herself, as well as society's toxic reaction to it, an odyssey that forms the bulk of the novel.

As for Stephen's qualities, throughout the story her actions reveal a woman of principle who confronts society's injustices and weathers its disdain. At the same time, they betray a woman who is unable to fully accept her own sexuality. Again, it must be kept in mind that the author was, to an extent, a reflection of her time.

"I'm some awful mistake—God's mistake," Stephen utters at one point. "I don't know if there are any more like me, I pray not, for their sakes, because it's pure hell."[4]

Still, despite her confusion and profound misgivings, Stephen con-tinues exploring her sexuality. In the process, she leaves her provin-cial village to pursue a literary career in London, then later moves to Paris. In time, she becomes an ambulance driver in occupied France during World War I, for which she is awarded the Croix de Guerre for her valor. More important, while in the ambulance corps, she falls in love with a virginal young woman named Mary. When this love inter-est begins returning her affection, however, Stephen, out of a sense of protectiveness, feels she must warn the woman about the stigma of gay affection.

"I am one of those whom God marked on the forehead," she tells her adoring companion. "Like Cain, I am marked and blemished."[5]

Stephen then explains to the young woman the high cost of same-sex love, while, at the same time, denouncing the hypocrisy of hetero-sexual society as she strives to bond with Mary. Her effort is to no avail, however. Mary, in the end, rejects Stephen for Martin, the man whose marriage proposal Stephen declined at the beginning of the story. This agonizing turn of events comprises an important theme of the book, one the author believes is inevitable: homosexual love, be-cause it does not lead to reproduction, continually loses out to hetero-sexual love.

As for sex, *The Well of Loneliness,* similar to other British novels of the period, merely suggests it. Although two female characters, at one point, do kiss, the book is not a steamy romance. Its few love scenes are never explicit or torrid, nor even particularly sexual. Rather than describing two women making love, for instance, they are por-trayed as being "in the grip of Creation." This is because John intended *The Well of Loneliness* to be an ethical treatise, not an erotic potboiler. In a letter to an American acquaintance, she said that she wrote the book to encourage homosexuals "to face up to a hostile world in their true colors, and this with dignity and courage."[6]

To this end, the novel concludes with Stephen's impassioned plea for justice:

> "God," she gasped, "we believe; we have told You we believe. . . . We have not denied You, then rise up and defend us. Acknowledge us, oh God, before the whole world. Give us also the right to our existence!"[7]

Ultimately, *The Well of Loneliness,* as a literary work, is a heartfelt yet strenuous novel brimming with angst, indignation, and a plethora of allusions to Christ and the martyrdom of the saints. In its day, however, it was more than a work of fiction. It was a daring manifesto, a call for tolerance of gays and lesbians, as well as a book designed to induce guilt in heterosexual readers, an effort to shame traditional British society. The response it received from publishers, however, as with its eventual treatment by the courts, proved to be altogether different.

Reviews and Rejoinders

When John's agent sent *The Well of Loneliness* to Cassell, the British publishing house that had an option on her next work, it declined the manuscript, as did succeeding publishers. This was because the lesbians in the story were depicted as society's victims, not its villains, an innovative approach publishers found too extreme. Similar reactions were encountered on the other side of the Atlantic as well. When an American publisher was being sought, the manuscript was turned down by Doubleday, Harpers, and Houghton Mifflin. Finally, publisher Jonathan Cape in London, impressed by the author's integrity, conviction, and especially her sales record, arranged for a British printing, while Blanche Knopf, business partner of husband Alfred, struck a deal for an American printing. An initial print run of 5,200 was ordered for the British edition, with the American version still to come. In July 1928, *The Well of Loneliness* was released to great fanfare and received reviews that were decidedly mixed.

"Finely conceived and finely written," is how the *Daily Telegraph* described the book. Others chose specific elements of the novel to compliment, such as the *Sunday Times*, which lauded the book's vibrant characterizations. Some critics were unimpressed, however. "Absolutely humorless," read the review in *The New Statesman*. "A failure," groused Leonard Woolf, husband of novelist Virginia Woolf, in a critique for *The Nation*.[8]

Still, contradictory reviews notwithstanding, books were sold. Sales were so strong, in fact, that a third printing was ordered in August, merely a month after the book's release. Then came the *Sunday Express* editorial by James Douglas, the one cited at the beginning of this chapter in which he declared it preferable to give children poison rather than *The Well of Loneliness*. When his article hit the newsstands, Douglas's comments, as well as Jonathan Cape's reckless reaction to them, propelled the book onto an entirely unforeseen path.

In Douglas's electrifying piece, which his adversaries accused him of writing mainly to publicize himself and his newspaper, the bombastic editor mocked the somberness of the novel and accused the book of endangering the morality of the nation. Launching into his attack full-frontal, Douglas shrewdly did not dispute the book's literary merits; rather, he conceded its artistry, then recast it as malevolence in disguise. More important, he opposed the novel's premise that lesbianism, for many women, is an inborn propensity that can lead to healthy, nourishing relationships if society does not interfere. Douglas not only disagreed with this idea, he disapproved of the author's mere expression of it.

Naturally, public reaction to his invective was swift and sweeping, as he had no doubt calculated. Certainly, the publicity caused the book to become the talk of London, and not in a favorable sense.

In response, publisher Jonathan Cape, without consulting either the author or her agent, dispatched to Britain's Home Secretary a copy of the novel and a selection of its better reviews for appraisal. He informed the Secretary that, if he wished, he was free to forward the book to the Director of Public Prosecutions for his consideration as well. Cape was confident the authorities would deem the novel suitable for public consumption. He then dashed off an open letter to James Douglas, notifying the editor that the novel had been submitted voluntarily to members of the government for review. The letter explained that, should the government find the book offensive, the publishing house would withdraw it from bookstores. He stressed, however, that the book would not be withdrawn simply because the editor of the *Sunday Express* happened to disapprove of it.

Within forty-eight hours came the official reply. To Cape's shock, the Home Secretary, Sir William Joynson-Hicks, had read the book and professed to be appalled by it. Even more distressing, Joynson-Hicks took it upon himself to send copies to those members of the judiciary he believed would be most inclined to condemn it should the book ever reach the courts, a preemptive strike that should have come as no surprise given the Home Secretary's reputation.

Besides being a government figure, Joynson-Hicks was the president of the Zenana Bible Mission and a staunch traditionalist who was forever crusading for a more virtuous society. It was he and his wife who had formed the Street Offences Committee, a group known for hounding London's prostitutes. He had also organized scores of raids on nightclubs and betting parlors over the years. At one point, he had even succeeded in having the Communist Party banned in Britain. To be sure, placing *The Well of Loneliness* in this man's hands was a major blunder, one for which its publisher, as well as its author, would pay dearly.

In his brusque letter to Jonathan Cape, the Home Secretary informed the publisher that the novel was dangerous to the public, and, for this reason, could be legally suppressed. He added, however, that since Cape had agreed to withdraw the book if requested, the government was now asking him to do just that.

In an outward show of compliance, Cape agreed immediately, directing his staff to halt the printing of the novel. He did something else, however. A month later, he arranged for *The Well of Loneliness* to be reprinted in its original form by Pegasus Press in Paris, then routed back to Britain for sale. He shipped duplicates of the book's molds to its new publisher without delay, then found a bookseller in London to serve as the novel's distributor when the stock arrived from France. Since British officials had not formally banned the book but merely requested that Cape's company no longer manufacture and dispense it, technically he was behaving within the law by arranging for a foreign agency to produce it. Pegasus Press set to work publishing and advertising the novel in British bookstores.

It was at this point that James Douglas returned to the fray. In an October article, the editor complained of seeing advertisements for

The Well of Loneliness in London bookshops, as well as copies of the book itself. He added, correctly, that the novel was now being published by a French company, and demanded to know what action, if any, the British government intended to take.

Naturally, given the very public nature of Douglas's challenge, the government had little choice but to act, so it directed the police to raid Cape's offices and those of the bookseller serving as the novel's British distributor and seize all unsold copies of the book. This heavy-handed action proved to be very unpopular with the citizenry, with accusations of government censorship abounding since authorities were confiscating a book that had not been legally prohibited. At the same time, demand for the novel was soaring—the scandal was creating quite a buzz—but unfortunately there were few copies to be had due to the government's efforts to block its availability. This frustrated the book-buying public, not to mention the publisher and author. Everyone, it seems, was upset by some aspect of the affair.

It was mainly for this reason that the judiciary decided to establish, once and for all, whether *The Well of Loneliness* constituted an "obscene libel." To this end, the court served Jonathan Cape and the British representative of Pegasus Press with summonses, although it did not charge them with misconduct. The court simply ordered them to appear so they could explain why, in their opinion, the novel should not be banned. As for John, she was not summoned at all, even though she was the creator of the work. The bench did not wish to hear from her, it said, because it was the novel that was on trial, not the author. If the book were to be ruled pornographic, it could be lawfully prohibited in Britain, which, at last, would bring an end to the whole awkward business. This is precisely what the court set out to do.

THE BRITISH TRIALS

The proceedings began on a chilly autumn morning in London. The courtroom was jammed; the trial was a sensational affair that focused on forbidden sex and artistic freedom. A substantial number of those in attendance were witnesses for the defense, luminaries in the arts and sciences who came to speak on behalf of *The Well of Loneliness*. The press was present as well, drawn to the controversial and consequential nature of the case, and to the celebrities filling the courtroom.

As for the principal players in the drama, the chief magistrate was Sir Chartres Biron, a man with a lifelong history of social traditionalism and a lackluster legal career. The prosecution consisted of conservative attorneys Eustace Fulton and Vincent Evans, while the defense was headed by Harold Rubenstein and Norman Birkett. Both defense attorneys were political liberals who were highly regarded in London legal circles. Birkett eventually served as a justice in the Nuremberg Trials. At issue was the subject matter of *The Well of Loneliness,* and whether the government's seizure of the novel from the offices of Jonathan Cape and Pegasus' British distributor was justified. Although same-sex relations between women were legal at the time, it was unclear whether publishing a book about lesbianism was likewise legal. This was the question to be answered.

The prosecution opened by stating its case, namely, that the topic of *The Well of Loneliness*—love between women—was an obscene one, and therefore the book itself was indecent. Homosexuality, the prosecutor insisted, should be discussed only in medical textbooks. In no case should it be mentioned in popular works, since the reading public could be damaged by such knowledge.

The prosecuting attorney then called to the stand the Scotland Yard inspector who had been present when the novel was confiscated a few weeks earlier. Asked to give his opinion of the book, the inspector replied that the book was obscene because it dealt with an obscene topic. He did not find fault with the actual text itself, however, which would have been rather hard for him to do given that it contained no sexually explicit scenes. Instead, the mere fact that the story involved women in love was sufficient, to his way of thinking, to render it pornographic. With this single piece of testimony, the prosecuting attorney concluded his argument. Warning that *The Well of Loneliness* was dangerous because it carried the potential to corrupt the receptive minds of British youth and other impressionable citizens, he demanded that it be barred from the libraries and bookshops of Britain.

Next came the argument for the defense. Attorney Birkett began by stating that nowhere in *The Well of Loneliness* could one find a single obscenity. Rather, the book was a work of art, he insisted. Birkett then announced his plan to call to the stand a large number of experts from all walks of life who would testify to the book's integrity.

Certainly it was true; Birkett had assembled a dazzling array of witnesses. Over forty eminent men and women had gathered in the courtroom to speak to the merits of *The Well of Loneliness,* among them physicians, educators, journalists, ministers, social workers, biologists, and booksellers. Also present were renowned authors such as D. H. Lawrence, Virginia Woolf, and Vita Sackville-West, although several writers chose not to come forward due to the scandalous nature of the trial. For his part, Bernard Shaw, although supportive, begged out of appearing because he considered himself to be highly immoral and failed to see what purpose his testimony would serve. Similarly, Noel Coward, while sympathetic toward John and her novel, preferred not to be present in a court of law, saying it was not his style. Then there was E. M. Forster, author of several notable works including the gay-themed *Maurice,* who was, from the beginning, enthusiastic about helping defend John and her book—that is, until she reprimanded him for failing to call her a "genius" in a letter of support he had composed for her. Thereafter, Forster was far less supportive, even going so far as to dismiss *The Well of Loneliness* as "tedious" in subsequent years. Still, despite such rows, a collection of illustrious people were on hand to make known their support for the novel and, more important, for the right of this or any other work of fiction to be available to the British people.

Then came a judicial action that altered the course of the trial. When the defense attorney asked his first witness to comment on the book's value, the magistrate interrupted and ordered him to stop. As for the issue facing the court—the question of whether the novel was obscene—the magistrate declared, "I don't think people are entitled to express an opinion."[9]

Startled, the attorney repeated that the witnesses were experts in literature, sexual behavior, ethics, and the like.

"I reject them all," the magistrate reiterated.[10] While *The Well of Loneliness* might indeed possess genuine literary qualities, he said, these were "defaced (by) certain deplorable lapses in taste."[11]

It was evident the magistrate was unreceptive to the defense's argument, so Birkett quickly wrapped up his presentation. There followed a one-week break so the bench could consider the evidence, such as it was.

When the trial resumed, the situation was as hopeless as ever. Again, expert testimony from the defense was disallowed, and, as before, the author, publisher, and distributor were not called to testify. Instead, the magistrate announced that he had arrived at a judgment about the novel, and his decision was to suppress it. As for his justification, he explained that although the lesbian characters in the story clearly displayed "horrible tendencies," the text did not hold them responsible.[12] More than that, the book portrayed them as attractive, kindhearted people.

And that, in a nutshell, was the problem. There is reason to believe the novel's opponents, including the magistrate himself, were not really perturbed because the book involved love between women. They were upset because its lesbians did not apologize for being gay, or, alternatively, did not come to a bad end. To be sure, to the male-centric power structure of post-Victorian society, the prospect that some women might get along quite well without men was perceived as an affront.

Outraged by the injustice, John jumped to her feet and addressed the magistrate directly without first seeking the court's permission.

"I protest! I emphatically protest!" she shouted. In short order, the magistrate ordered her to shut up and sit down.[13]

Apparently hoping to put a quick end to the increasingly unpopular and unruly ordeal, the magistrate asserted that *The Well of Loneliness* was indisputably obscene and that the government had behaved properly in confiscating it. He ordered the remaining stock to be incinerated "in the King's furnace" and commanded Jonathan Cape and the British distributor to pay fines.[14] In this way, the court effectively banned the novel and punished those businessmen who brought it to the public.

Of course, it was obvious to everyone that the trial had been a farce from the start. The magistrate and prosecutors, along with newspaper editor James Douglas, were longtime acquaintances and political cronies who, it appears, had discussed the case well in advance of its court date and were in agreement about its deserved outcome. Although these men achieved the result they desired, they did so at some expense to themselves and the reputation of the judiciary. Because the press covered the spectacle so thoroughly, the public got to see a disturbing feature of its legal system; its lack of fairness regarding same-sex issues at a time when British society was otherwise becoming more tolerant of lesbianism.

Even more dismaying to writers, in particular, was the fact that the court attacked an author's right to compose a work about a subject that made the court uncomfortable. The judiciary, it seems, was unable to grasp the difference that exists between the theme of a novel and an author's treatment of that theme. As several observers pointed out at the time, the Holy Bible is rife with sin and depravity, and yet it is considered a sacred book because its motif is one of salvation. Likewise, Shakespeare's plays are replete with unorthodox figures and disputable actions, but are considered works of art and enshrined as major cultural achievements. A topic may be presented in myriad ways, they argued; it is only the presentation itself that should be judged decent or indecent. Because of the court's ignorance of this simple distinction, however, many writers, already skeptical of the British legal establishment, found their cynicism heightened.

As for John, she was exasperated and disappointed by the trial and afterward sought solace from friends and allies in the literary world. Her lawyers, meanwhile, requested an appeal in an effort to persuade a higher court to overturn the lower court's decision regarding the confiscation of *The Well of Loneliness*. The judiciary recognized their right to an appeal, but scheduled the hearing for two weeks later, thereby ensuring that the defense would have little time to prepare for it.

The Appeal

On December 14, 1928, the proceedings commenced at the Court of London Sessions with the eighty-seven-year-old Sir Robert Wallace presiding. A dozen magistrates assembled to hear the case, two of whom were women. Potential witnesses included novelist Rudyard Kipling, who was on hand to testify on behalf of the prosecution, because, he said, lesbianism was revolting and writing about it only made it worse. It was probably no accident that he was also a personal friend and occasional houseguest of Sir William Joynson-Hicks, the Home Secretary who had been the first official to condemn the book. In any event, Kipling was not called to testify, nor was anyone else for that matter, since the court again excluded witnesses.

Also disturbing was the court's lack of familiarity with *The Well of Loneliness* itself. Prior to the appeal, Cape sought permission to supply the twelve magistrates with copies of the novel so they would have sufficient time to read it before the trial. The chairman of the court, however, decided the proposal was "neither appropriate nor practicable," and refused to give the magistrates such easy access to the book.

The hearing opened with the solicitor general reading aloud isolated passages from *The Well of Loneliness*. Although it was evident that the excerpts, even when taken out of context, were in no way lewd, the lawyer worked hard to suggest otherwise. After he finished, he faced the magistrates and declared the gay love story to be "more subtle, demoralizing, corrosive, corruptive, than anything that was ever written."[15] He further concluded that the lower court had been correct in classifying the novel obscene and dangerous to society.

The defense team then presented its case. John's lawyers reminded the magistrates that love between women was a fact of life and for this reason warranted exploration in literature. They also stressed the intelligence and artistry of John's writing, as well as the need for the public to have unfettered access to fine literary works on an array of subjects from diverse viewpoints. At last, when both sides had presented their arguments, the magistrates retired to consider the verdict. Five minutes later, to the astonishment of spectators, they returned with their judgment. The bench upheld the lower court's ruling against Jonathan Cape and the Pegasus distributor, maintaining the book could "deprave and corrupt" those of timid, influential mind.

"Put in a word," Sir Wallace said, "this is a disgusting book."[16]

With this moralistic pronouncement, the domestic trials for *The Well of Loneliness* came to an end. The novel was officially proscribed in Britain, and although a group of distinguished writers gathered afterward to protest the decision, their efforts were futile. The book remained banned for the next thirty years.

THE AMERICAN TRIAL

The book's progress in the United States, in the meantime, faced another set of obstacles. The first problem centered on the wrath of Blanche Knopf, who had arranged to publish the American edition of the book. Knopf had followed the controversy in England from the beginning and was perturbed by that nation's repressive actions against the novel. Even more, she was angered at Jonathan Cape's willingness to withdraw the book from circulation. Most of all, she was incensed at John for not objecting to Cape's actions. In a letter dated September 27, 1928, Knopf scolded the author for not holding the publisher to his contract.

"You made no attempt to make him carry out the terms of his agreement with you," she said, adding that, as the book's future American publisher, she was troubled by John's inaction.[17] Knopf went on to say that she fully expected controversy to erupt upon the novel's release in the United States and was concerned her company would be confronted with the demoralizing prospect of fighting for a book that had not been defended in its own homeland. Clearly piqued, she concluded her letter by canceling her deal with John. *The Well of Loneliness* would have to find another American publisher.

Shortly thereafter it did. Two New Yorkers with substantial experience in the industry, Pascal Covici and Donald Friede, quickly joined forces to produce it. Offering John a sizable advance and pricing the book at twice the usual cost, they placed the novel on the U.S. market in December 1928, and sales took off instantly. Within its first month, over 20,000 copies were sold, aiming it toward best-seller status. A month later, the book went into its sixth printing. To be sure, the American public was hungry for the daring novel, although a group called the New York Society for the Suppression of Vice was not.

When the book first appeared on the shelves, the organization demanded that bookshops and department stores, most notably Macys, stop selling it or risk legal action. The stores ignored the threat, however, so a few weeks later the Society concocted a new strategy, one that would prove more successful. Claiming that a dozen citizens had complained to them about the allegedly pornographic work, the Society prompted a police raid of the offices of Covici and Friede. The result was another obscenity trial, *The People of New York vs. Donald Friede and Covici-Friede.*

The proceedings commenced on April 8, 1929, in New York City, with three judges hearing the case. The prosecution included John Sumner, the Secretary of the New York Society for the Suppression of Vice, while the defense was led by Morris Ernst, a liberal with a strong interest in constitutional law and a commitment to freedom of speech. Highly regarded by his peers, Ernst eventually became renowned for tackling tough censorship cases. As for *The Well of Lone-*

liness, he decided to approach the matter not by pleading for the tolerance of lesbianism but by presenting the issue as a breach of authors' rights; a smart move in a nation founded on the freedom of expression.

Attorney Sumner began by reading aloud several excerpts from the novel, passages he claimed offended one's moral sensibilities. He was attempting to duplicate the successful British strategy of portraying the work as indecent and therefore hazardous to the public. The justices listened attentively as he made his case.

Then came the defense attorney's argument. Ernst opened by stating that obscenity can be found in almost any book if a reader searches diligently enough, and that most anything can be construed as offensive if that is one's intention. He next declared that *The Well of Loneliness* was literature, not pornography, and to support his assertion pointed to a letter of support for the novel signed by, among others, Ernest Hemingway, Upton Sinclair, and F. Scott Fitzgerald. He also read aloud a sample of glowing reviews from respected American newspapers, thereby countering the prosecution's efforts to depict the novel as carnal rubbish.

He continued building his case. Ernst argued that the novel dealt with an important social issue—same-sex affection—and that it is preferable to address such a matter directly rather than try to suppress it. It is through the free exchange of ideas, he insisted, not through enforced silence, that a democracy confronts and resolves thorny issues, this being the key to genuine social progress. He also stated that the novel had been discriminated against merely because it involved two women. Had the story centered on a man and a woman, he said, it would not have been considered controversial. Finally, he called to the stand several expert witnesses.

After eliciting their testimony, Ernst concluded by stating that, in the United States, an author has the fundamental right to express himself or herself, and that it is not the government's role to dictate which ideas may be expressed in print and which may not. With this, the defense rested its case.

The justices then assigned themselves an eleven-day term to read *The Well of Loneliness* and consider the arguments. On the ninth of April, they returned with their verdict, a ruling stating that it was not the job of the court to decide matters of literary taste; rather, its purpose was to determine whether a literary work violated existing obscenity laws. In this regard, the verdict asserted that *The Well of Lone-liness* did not, in fact, infringe any laws.

Thus, the novel was now officially legal in the United States, the trial having been brisk, decisive, and indisputably objective. This stood in stark contrast to the earlier British proceedings.

Whereas the British trial had been structured in such a way as to guarantee the novel would be ruled obscene, the American trial was conducted properly, in accordance with established legal procedure, and with both sides granted the opportunity to present their arguments. This included the use of expert witnesses. Also, the American judges, unlike the British magistrates who were unacquainted with the novel, read the book before ruling on it. Furthermore, while the British court used its highly visible position to bad-mouth the novel and humiliate its author and publisher, the American court refused to pan the work or embarrass anyone associated with it, even going so far as to state, for the record, that this was not its role. As a result, the aftermath was minimal—the novel continued being sold in the United States, the controversy was put to rest—while the aftershocks of the British proceedings were far-reaching and protracted.

SOCIAL AND POLITICAL IMPACT OF THE OBSCENITY TRIALS

The British trials, for several years thereafter, carried repercussions for the literary community as well as the gay and lesbian citizenry. The proceedings also had an impact on the judiciary, with legal experts, decades later, continuing to examine the marred *Well of Loneliness* trials, believing there was much to be learned from them.

John reacted by becoming ill at the conclusion of the ordeal, due presumably to the cumulative effects of prolonged stress. Some biographers have even attempted to tie her development of several illnesses in the subsequent years—especially the onset of inoperable cancer twenty years later—to the strain of the proceedings, but this claim, while compelling, is unconvincing. That said, there is little doubt that her tribulations took a heavy toll. A principled woman who considered herself morally superior to her detractors, John was deeply hurt by their public attempts to depict her as vulgar and corrupt. So distressed was she, in fact, that her next novel dealt expressly with the suffering of Christ, with whom she readily identified. One topic about which she never wrote again, however, was lesbianism—nor, for that matter, did any other British author for many years to come.

Whereas *The Well of Loneliness,* in a more flexible society, might have paved the way for further works about women in love, the judiciary's authoritarian action against the novel quashed any chance of this happening in Britain. Writers, chilled by the legal events, were unwilling to pen a manuscript they believed publishers would reject for fear that a court would block its publication. As well, they were loath to risk the kind of national drubbing endured by John, her reputation having been damaged, in some quarters, by charges of immorality.

The trials also had a negative impact on gay life itself, casting a shadow over the daily routines of many homosexual men and women. Inasmuch as British society was developing a greater understanding and tolerance of those who were gay and lesbian in the 1920s, the court's blaring denunciation of *The Well of Loneliness* and the intense public debate triggered by the scandal caused many ordinary homosexual citizens to become uncomfortable and self-conscious. Although there was no official crackdown—there was, for instance, no notable rise in the number of gay-related arrests during this period—lesbians and gay men, most notably those who were not members of the privileged class, became more guarded in their relationships. Their caution was not unwarranted. Close friendships among unmarried women, in particular, came to be viewed with suspicion, especially when they involved so-called spinsters, in what was to become the major "lesbian scare" of the era. In such ways, the obscenity trials disrupted gay life and slowed the headway lesbians and gay men had heretofore made.

"The government stigmatized and criminalized a kind of love," says writer Diana Souhami. "Its idiocy echoed down the years, silencing writers, consigning people to concealment of their deepest feelings and to public scorn."[18] Unfortunately, it would be quite some time before the gay citizenry would return to its previous course of social and political progress.

This is not to say, however, that the affair was wholly without value. It did, in fact, yield certain benefits. The enormous publicity generated by newspaper editor James Douglas's attack on the book sparked enormous sales, with demand for the novel increasing even further as it faced official prohibition. The book sold well in France, too, largely because the French press publicized the British quarrel surrounding it. Meanwhile, in the United States, the novel's American obscenity trial also made headlines, pushing sales upward. Thus, the attention *The Well of Loneliness* received—coverage, many critics maintained, that went far beyond that merited by the quality of the work itself—propelled both the book and its author, at least momentarily, to international fame.

As a result, the situation allowed John to earn a sizable sum of money, but even more important to her, it ushered the topic of lesbianism into greater public discourse. Newspapers now covered the subject to an extent previously unseen in the British press. In a letter to the editor of a London daily, one reader, referring to the novel's extensive coverage, wrote that the actions of Douglas and the patriarchal British judiciary caused the topic of same-sex love to be "inquired into and pleasingly investigated as never before in the history of this our hypocritical country."[19] By all accounts, the media coverage did serve to increase public awareness and discussion of same-sex issues.

In addition, the novel and its hardships fueled Britain's censorship controversy. For quite some time, debate had raged about the government's role in the arts, with many accusing the authorities of wielding too much power in deciding what the populace could see, hear, and read. With the advent of *The Well of Loneliness* trials, new concerns were voiced and innovative arguments were made, as were demands that existing censorship laws be modified. Although change in these laws was not immediately forthcoming, the case for such revision did gain strength as a result of the novel's ordeal. Eventually, change was achieved.

Thirty years later, the British government revisited *The Well of Loneliness* proceedings at a time when the legal system was upgrading its obscenity laws. The aim was to clarify the criteria used when evaluating a written work's suitability for public availability; specifically, whether artistic quality and social value should be included in the equation. The court's refusal to hear expert testimony on such matters during the earlier *Well of Loneliness* trials had been widely perceived as unjust. By disallowing the considered opinions of those most knowledgeable about these areas, the court had given itself a black eye. Accordingly, the government, in 1959, approved the Obscene Publications Act, which stated unequivocally that a book's artistic worth and social import should henceforth be taken into consideration. Moreover, this new legislation was promptly put to use in the trial of *Lady Chatterley's Lover,* in which the controversial novel, to the cheers of courtroom spectators, was ruled suitable for public consumption.

In the end, then, John prevailed in her struggle, her efforts ultimately easing the way for modern gay and lesbian writers to publish their work without undue governmental interference. As for *The Well of Loneliness,* it is still in print today, available in several languages, and obtainable throughout the world, including Britain, where it is rightfully considered a landmark work by a courageous, passionate, and principled woman.

Chapter 4

A Case of Espionage:
Guy Burgess, Donald Maclean, and the "Ring of Five"

In May 1951, soon after the onset of the Cold War, an event took place that shook the leaders of the Western world and unnerved the general public. It involved the abrupt disappearance of a pair of British diplomats, Guy Burgess and Donald Maclean; two upper-class, Cambridge-educated men with lengthy, high profile careers.

"Vanishing Act Throws Big Scare into British," blared the headlines of the *World Telegraph,* and it certainly was true.[1] Concern erupted at once over their disappearance, the fear being that they had been kidnapped, or, worse still, assassinated. There were also murmurs of a drinking binge gone awry, possibly a fatal accident. Two weeks after the men's disappearance, however, the truth began to emerge, and it was excruciating: the statesmen, it seems, were actually KGB operatives who, for twenty years, had been supplying the Kremlin with mounds of top secret intelligence material smuggled out of Britain and the United States. Under threat of exposure, they defected to the Soviet Union, hurrying away at midnight on a steamer to Saint-Malo, France, and were later ushered to Moscow. And there was another bombshell: Burgess and Maclean, the world soon discovered, were gay; this, during an era when homosexuality, like treason, was viewed with outright contempt. Thus began one of the most riveting spy scandals of the century, an affair that disrupted international relations and triggered in Britain and the United States a witch-hunt against the gay and lesbian citizenry, thereby intensifying the already paranoid atmosphere of the Cold War itself.

THE CAMBRIDGE YEARS

Burgess and Maclean first met in 1931 as undergraduates at Cambridge University. Maclean—tall, sandy-haired, and plump in those days—came from a privileged background. His father, Sir Donald Maclean, was the Deputy Speaker of the House of Commons and the eventual leader of the Liberal Party. The elder Maclean was also something of a tyrant, however, a man known, among other things, for being distant and uncompromising toward his family. Rumor had it that he insisted his son attend a preparatory school so strict that the boys' pants pockets were sewn shut so they could not touch themselves.[2] Moreover, the school's headmaster, said to be engrossed in "a fanatical pursuit of purity," refused to let the students participate in contact sports "in case the boys were contaminated."[3] In such ways, the senior Maclean, stoic and severe, in conjunction with the prohibitive school he chose for his son, produced an insecure and deeply inhibited young man. Still, despite his timidity, young Maclean eventually competed for, and won, a scholarship to Cambridge where he registered to study foreign languages.

Burgess, by comparison, was confident, boisterous, and opinionated. Described as having blue eyes, full lips, curly hair, and an attentive face, he emerged from a distinctive background as well. Although he was only thirteen years old when his father died, Burgess' mother, affluent and ambitious, managed to send him to Eton, where his young classmates considered him "sophisticated, at ease, with a cool detached manner, an intellectually superior being."[4]

While he was at Eton, Burgess began developing strong political convictions. The school, providentially, hosted a lecture by a union organizer, a dynamic man who spoke at length about Britain's streets of poverty. To the sheltered Burgess, unaware of such brutal economic realities, the message was an epiphany. So moved was he, in fact, that he thereafter approached the world from a leftist perspective, especially a few years later when, like Maclean, he was awarded a scholarship to attend Cambridge. It was there that Burgess set out to immerse himself in Marxism, convinced that this ideology offered the solution to Britain' s growing destitution.

To this end, the young firebrand formed a circle of friends during his first year at college, fellow students who, like himself, held strong left-wing beliefs. Soon, the members of this clique came to include

Anthony Blunt, Harold "Kim" Philby, John Cairncross, and the unassuming Maclean, who relished the group's opposition to his father's Liberal Party. In time, this coterie would become known as the "Ring of Five."

Burgess also pursued sex during this time, and always with other men. As with many students and several Cambridge dons, he was known, in the parlance of the times, as a "confirmed homosexual."

"Guy never troubled to conceal his indifference to women and his preference for boys, with whom he paraded in the streets of Cambridge under the increasingly unconvincing pretext that they were his nephews," writes John Fisher, a former diplomatic correspondent.[5] At times, Burgess's lovers also included members of his left-wing group, Maclean becoming one such partner before long. Several decades later, when the two men were no longer on speaking terms, Burgess denied ever having had sex with Maclean, saying, "It would be like going to bed with a great white woman." In any event, there is reason to believe they were, during their student years at any rate, kindred spirits who shared a cocktail of erotic desire and revolutionary politics.[6] It has even been suggested that Burgess, in those early days, used sex to entice Maclean to Marxism. Whatever the truth of the matter, it is known that their friendship was bolstered in 1932 when they joined an unofficial study group at Cambridge so they could learn more about communist ideology. Shortly thereafter, the two impassioned, impressionable idealists came to the attention of KGB recruiters, a turn of events that would change the young men's lives forever.

One of those recruiters, a Hungarian named Teodor Maly, was a former priest who had become a KGB agent after being imprisoned, while still a clergyman, by Czarist troops earlier in the century. Awakened to the political realities of Central Europe, he subsequently devoted himself to helping build through communism what he believed would be a more equitable world. Similar convictions were held by his Austrian accomplice, Arnold Deutsch, with whom he scoured British colleges searching for optimistic young minds receptive to their brand of politics. Moreover, they found, over and again, that many people were indeed willing to consider their unconventional views because the mood of the times was one of desperation.

The Great Depression, it seems, had hit hard in Britain; unemployment was rampant and food was scarce. As in the United States, there were bread lines. In addition, hunger marches were staged by impoverished coal miners. Consequently, many students who possessed social consciences and rebellious natures observed these conditions and found them appalling. More than that, they felt the Depression proved their parents' way of doing things was wrong; that capitalism, as an economic, social, and political system, was a washout. Communism, on the other hand, offered the promise of a new and better tomorrow, a time when everyone's needs would be fulfilled, not just those of the upper class. Of course, this was before the world had the opportunity to bear witness to Josef Stalin's lethal purges, to the gloom and dehumanization of daily life in a Marxist society, and to other stark evidence of communism's bankruptcy when put into actual practice. During this more innocent age, a substantial share of the citizenry, particularly university students, looked to communism with genuine hope. Such guileless, idealistic youths as Burgess and Maclean excited Maly and Deutsch's interest, and in the Ring of Five they discovered a ready-made collection of such young people.

In this manner, Donald Maclean, during his stint at Cambridge, came to Maly's attention, and the agent at once concentrated his energies on recruiting him. Deutsch, meanwhile, set out to entice the other members of the clique. At this preliminary stage, the agents did not inform their prey that they were being enlisted by the Soviet government for work with the KGB. Instead, they were told they would be performing covert tasks for the Comintern, a comparatively respectable international Communist organization. In due time and with persistent coaxing, all of the young men agreed to participate; one of the men in particular was especially eager to comply: Guy Burgess, whose enthusiasm could probably have been foreseen given the leftist views he had embraced so fervently since his Eton days.

The Burgess Path

While being groomed as an operative, Burgess continued studying history at Cambridge. So captivated was he by the ambiance of the scholarly community, in fact, that he remained there for two more years after graduation, serving as a researcher and lecturer in history while awaiting a formal fellowship. During this period, the spirited revolutionary also continued romancing attractive young men and communist ideals with equal passion. As for the former, his tastes ran toward the proletariat.

"Burgess found lovers in every social category," says Yuri Modin, his KGB controller, adding that Burgess "had a strong preference for lorry drivers and other working men."[7]

In terms of his political activities, the young communist routinely involved himself in virtually any situation he found unjust. Among other interventions, Burgess helped organize a strike for waiters who worked in the Cambridge dining halls, because he felt the university system treated them unjustly. Furthermore, his efforts were successful in that the waiters' pay, as well as their work schedules, were eventually upgraded. Still, despite such victories for university waiters, Burgess' years at Cambridge were destined to come to an end when, in 1935, the KGB ordered him to find a more useful venue, one where he could obtain intelligence information for the Kremlin. To this end, he bid farewell to colleagues in the ivory tower and ventured into the larger world.

Initially, he hoped to penetrate the British Conservative Party itself, and thus applied for several jobs within the Tory system. Burgess' efforts, however, proved to be in vain. Unfortunately for him, the Conservatives were disturbed by his student activities as an ardent Communist, despite the fact that he had, at the behest of the KGB, publicly renounced his Marxist views for the sake of appearances. The Conservatives further disapproved of his heavy drinking and tousled appearance. Although they did not state it publicly, they also may have objected to his gay sex life, about which he was known to be very frank. Burgess, however, remained undaunted. Pushing aside their rebuffs, he redoubled his efforts to enter mainstream society and eventually succeeded in landing a job at the British Broadcasting Corporation (BBC), where he produced a radio program on topics of current interest.

As for his personal life, Burgess, despite his new and impressive position, continued living like a student. He wore the same clothing he had worn at Cambridge in years past and continued drinking and carousing as well.

"Accounts of his social life during this period agree that he was as rumbustious as ever," says historian Bruce Page. "His home away from home was the Reform Club where he was such a regular and devoted figure . . . that a specially large glass of port was christened, in his honor, a 'double Burgess.' "8

Furthermore, he was now a very busy man. At the same time he was producing his radio show at the BBC and pursuing a high-octane personal life, Burgess was also secretly working as a political free-lancer. Among other duties, he served as a courier to the leaders of the British and French governments; powerful men who were, at that moment, engaged in a crucial correspondence owing to the burgeoning Nazi threat in Europe. What these leaders did not know, however, is that Burgess, as their messenger, was methodically stopping at a London hotel en route, opening and photographing their documents, then handing over the film to Soviet agents to be smuggled to Moscow. As a result, the USSR had substantial knowledge of France and Britain's plans during the precarious years leading up to World War II. Burgess' good fortune as a spy persisted as a result.

In 1938, Britain's Secret Intelligence Service, impressed by his seeming patriotism, offered him a position in its agency. Burgess, of course, seized the opportunity at once, since it would provide him with a portal into the nation's intelligence network, a placement both he and the KGB had long desired. As for the job itself, it involved concocting anti-Nazi propaganda and arranging for it to be aired on underground radio stations across Europe, a task at which Burgess proved to be remarkably effective. He also helped organize a school for saboteurs, with training carried out by, among others, leftist revolutionaries experienced in such matters. In addition, he continued working for the KGB. Burgess's pro-Soviet activities, in fact, picked up sharply during this period because he now had access to far more valuable information. Moreover, as an ambitious young operative he dutifully followed established espionage procedure for getting this material into the right hands.

Two of his acquaintances, for instance, a married couple, recalled how he once telephoned them on a Sunday morning and invited them to lunch at a Chinese restaurant by the docks on the Thames. Upon their arrival, Burgess announced he had to drop off a letter, then dashed across the street and stuffed an envelope into the mail slot of a sailors' apparel shop. The couple, familiar with his sexual tastes, found the incident amusing, believing he was probably "in mid-affair with some deck-hand."9 But they were wrong. That particular area, it was later discovered, was a choice location for KGB "dead drops," information exchange sites, and Burgess apparently used this one quite often.

That all came to an end in 1940, however, when Winston Churchill became prime minister and set out to restructure the intelligence service. During the shakeup, many employees were let go, Guy Burgess among them.

"We never quite knew why he was dropped," says the KGB's Modin, "but I would speculate that it had something to do with his overt homosexuality."[10]

Whatever the reason, Burgess returned to the BBC, where he produced another well-regarded political program while waiting for his next covert operation. This assignment, it turns out, would take a few years to arrive.

It was 1944, and Burgess landed a job with the News Department of the British Foreign Office in London, where he soon became privy to all manner of information passing through the organization. Curiously, the Foreign Office did not conduct a formal security check before hiring him, believing, mistakenly, he had already passed such a screening when employed earlier by the Secret Intelligence Service. This was how Burgess came to be situated in a politically sensitive job despite his checkered past and was given unimpeded access to classified information useful to the Soviet Union. To Britain's benefit, though, it appears that his ability to function as a spy began to deteriorate at precisely this same time. By several accounts, he started drinking more heavily, became increasingly reckless with restricted documents, and, more than ever, pursued handsome young men with a vengeance.

To be sure, Burgess was strongly drawn to sex at this time, making "persistent and persuasive advances" toward most any man he believed was seducible, especially those who were young.[11] Furthermore, his London flat, decorated in a red, white, and blue Union Jack motif, became renowned in the neighborhood for the "drunken, striptease (strictly male) parties he held there."[12] This occurred while he was employed by the image-conscious Foreign Office.

Predictably perhaps, as the Cold War escalated, so did Burgess' alcohol consumption. By the late 1940s, he was also popping amphetamines on his way to work each morning and becoming even more lax with confidential documents. On one occasion, he was even reproached for passing around a snapshot of a new boyfriend during a

Foreign Office briefing. Increasingly uninhibited, Burgess now moved into a flat in Soho with a nineteen-year-old named Jack Hewit, a former dancer and cast member of *No, No, Nanette,* who he persuaded to perform minor espionage tasks. He also introduced him to Cambridge pal and occasional paramour Anthony Blunt, telling Hewit, without hesitation, that Blunt was a spy. Unquestionably, Burgess' behavior was becoming truly careless, if not downright dangerous, both on and off the job, thereby jeopardizing the information to which he had been entrusted by Britain and the Soviet Union.

As it stands, part of his decline may have been caused by, or at least hastened by, the drugs on which he had become dependent. According to a close friend, Burgess, at this point, was routinely using numerous substances:

> He was now perpetually taking sedatives to calm his nerves, and immediately followed them with stimulants in order to counteract their effect. . . . Combined with a large and steady intake of alcohol, the consumption of drugs, narcotics, sedatives, stimulants, barbiturates, sleeping pills, or *anything,* it seemed, so long as it would modify whatever he happened to be feeling any particular moment, produced an extraordinary and incalculable alteration of mood, so that one could not possibly tell what condition he would be in from one moment to the next.[13]

Thus, it came as no great shock to anyone when Burgess was abruptly transferred to what was believed to be a more benign, less visible position in the Department of Far Eastern Affairs at the Foreign Office. Just as his professional life was beginning to wind down, however, he was involved, in rapid succession, in three awkward episodes that sealed his professional fate.

For starters, he was pushed down a flight of stairs late one night while leaving The Gargoyle, a favorite nightspot, in the process fracturing his skull and breaking his jaw. Then, to recuperate, he and his mother went on holiday to Dublin, where he was involved in a car crash caused by his drinking. In the accident, a man was killed, a matter that was quickly silenced by the British government. Burgess then traveled to Tangier, where he remained intoxicated throughout his visit. Among other gaffes, he pointed out British operatives in public and made sexual overtures to young Moslem men on the street.

Finally, when he returned to his Foreign Office job several weeks later, Burgess found himself reassigned for the last time, to the post of Second Secretary at the British Embassy in Washington, DC. This new job, despite its prestigious location, would allow him no direct contact with the ambassador nor would it require of him any real work. In a word, he was being marginalized, but in such a way as to save face for all concerned.

As for the KGB, its faith in Burgess was waning as well, at least in certain quarters. Although his knowledge of history and contemporary politics was unequaled among his peers, and while he certainly had succeeded in furnishing the Kremlin with an astounding amount of valuable material over the years, Burgess's critics in Moscow were increasingly dismissing him as "a rogue, an adventurer, a liar and a drunk."[14]

Whatever his reputation, Burgess, before heading to the United States, decided to throw himself a going-away celebration at his Soho flat. A free-wheeling affair, it was reportedly attended by "fellow-Communists, spy-hunters, male prostitutes and other eccentric personalities."[15] As one of his colleagues, Hector MacNeil, was leaving the party, he jokingly cautioned Burgess to remember three important points when living in the United States: "Don't be too aggressively left-wing. Don't get involved in race relations; and above all, make sure that there aren't any homosexual incidents which might cause trouble." To which Burgess replied: "I understand Hector: what you mean is that I mustn't make a pass at Paul Robeson," a reference to the controversial black singer known for his extreme left-wing views.[16]

On that note, the discredited Guy Burgess left the next morning for Washington, DC. There he lived with fellow Ring of Five operative Kim Philby, who was now the British intelligence network's foremost liaison to the recently established Central Intelligence Agency. In this critical position, Philby had an opening to vital information shared by both nations, including their awareness—or lack of awareness—of the clandestine activities of his Cambridge comrades, Burgess and Maclean.

The Maclean Path

For his part, Donald Maclean had pursued a more conventional course after agreeing to assist the Communist cause. After his father's death in 1932, the shy young man blossomed, becoming self-assured and articulate while developing admirable writing and debating skills. During his remaining years at Cambridge, he joined a socialist student group and became its most forceful, yet eloquent, member. He also wrote an influential article for the *Cambridge Left,* a socialist review, predicting the downfall of capitalism. A true believer, Maclean's goal, after completing his studies, was to move to the USSR, where he would teach English to the Soviets so they could better communicate with Westerners. The KGB, however, had other plans for him. It felt the Communist movement would be better served if Maclean, like Burgess, were to publicly renounce his Marxist background, then penetrate the British government. In this way, he could help dismantle capitalist society from within. Maclean agreed to remain in Britain and infiltrate the government, although the assignment disappointed him deeply.

"He was never meant to live in the murky, constrained atmosphere of secret work," says his former KGB boss today.[17]

Regardless, the dutiful Maclean secured a position with the Foreign Office in London as Third Secretary, then soon was promoted to the British Embassy in Paris. Thus began his ascent. It was during this time that Maclean set out to reinvent himself, and, by all accounts, was strikingly successful in doing so. The pudgy young man became a trim and fit adult. He likewise refined his style of dress and presented himself confidently to the world. As a result, old friends, upon meeting him once again, were struck by his attractiveness and poise; in some respects, the image of Sir Donald himself, his late father.

"Maclean," recalls journalist Cyril Connolly, "seemed suddenly to have acquired a backbone, morally and physically. His appearance greatly improved . . . and he had become a personage."[18]

There was one feature of Maclean, however, that he could not suppress: his attraction to other men. As it was, he seldom dated women, and, when he did, it was not to his liking. "Donald in fact had no luck with the girls," offered one writer by way of explanation.[19] Luck, however, had nothing to do with it. Maclean was gay, and all the heterosexual dates in the world would not change that simple fact. Still, he was nothing if not determined. Perhaps realizing it would be expedient to have a wife if he hoped to advance fully in his diplomatic career, he did, in 1938, wed.

It was on a snowy December evening that he met his future bride, Melinda, at the Café de Flore on the Left Bank. A rich American who was four years his junior, she was, rather sporadically, a student at the Sorbonne.

"She was quite pretty and vivacious but rather reserved," recalled a friend of Maclean's who met her that same night. "Frankly, I thought she was a bit prim."[20]

Prudishness, however, could be a plus in a diplomat's wife, Maclean apparently decided, as could stylishness, tact, and other qualities Melinda possessed. Therefore, several months after meeing her he asked her to marry him. She did not, however, consent at once.

"Her letters home showed her ambivalence," recalls journalist Phillip Knightly. "On the one hand she was genuinely fond of him and liked the idea of marrying a diplomat from a titled family; on the other she had the feeling that he would be a difficult husband."[21]

Nevertheless, Melinda did eventually decide to marry the enigmatic young man, and so they wed, and at the eleventh hour. The ceremony, it seems, took place on the day foreign citizens such as themselves were ordered to depart from Paris because Nazi troops were amassing outside the city.

Upon returning to London to make their home, it soon became apparent that Maclean would indeed make a less than ideal husband. Perhaps by design, he found little time for his wife; a situation he attributed to the fact that war was near at hand and he was now very busy. Moreover, within a few weeks he began insisting that Melinda return to New York, where she could live more safely with her family if war did, in fact, erupt. Of course, this was a move not without positive consequences for Maclean himself. With his wife out of the picture, he would be free to pursue his own interests, whatever they might be. It is certainly true that after Melinda boarded the ship for the United States Maclean did become more mobile, although the nature and extent of his actions during this time have never been fully documented.

We do know, however, that from the late 1930s to the mid-1940s he drank heavily when not at work and sometimes disappeared for several days at a time. On such occasions, those close to him did not know if he was in some out-of-the-way area of London seeking same-sex love or lost or unconscious somewhere, the result of a drinking binge. Today we know he may have been conducting espionage missions, at least during some of those episodes. On one such occasion, for instance, Maclean was spotted in a Swiss village using an assumed name, presumably in the midst of a covert operation.

Despite such mysterious conduct, however, he continued to be highly regarded by his colleagues and superiors at the Foreign Office, who were completely in the dark about his espionage activities. As well, they knew nothing about his same-sex affections, and very little about his reliance on alcohol. Of course, this was no accident. Maclean went to great lengths to conceal these features of his life, including his drinking, which tended to loosen his tongue, the kiss of death to a spy.

"Only under the influence of drink would Maclean sometimes reveal glimpses of the dark, rebellious side of his mind," notes one observer. "That was why, to a far greater extent than Burgess, he tried not to mix business with pleasure, seldom going out with his Foreign Office colleagues."[22]

In 1944 Maclean was promoted to acting First Secretary, as well as acting Head of the Chancery at the British Embassy in Washington, DC, a considerable achievement given he was only thirty-one years old. Moreover, three years later he was appointed the British delegation's secretary to the newly created Combined Policy Committee, an immensely powerful group in place to formulate the nuclear policies of the United States, Canada, and Britain. While in this latter post, Maclean was most valuable to the Soviets.

According to a 1951 communiqué from the Chairman of the Atomic Energy Commission to FBI Director J. Edgar Hoover, Maclean, in that position, had access to vital information about the ability and willingness of the United States, Canada, and Britain to wage a nuclear war.[23] He knew the amount of uranium required to build an atomic bomb as well as the locations and costs of the ore itself. He was also privy to a secret arrangement between Western nations and South Africa in which uranium would be extracted from African gold deposits. He knew, as well, about the decision to launch the Manhattan Project.

"Some of the information available to Maclean in 1947-48," concluded the communiqué, "was classified Top Secret and would then have been of interest to the Soviet Union."[24]

Today, the Russians concede that this appraisal of Maclean's productivity was entirely correct: "It is no overstatement to say that the

KGB was able to follow the political evolution of the Western atomic program from its genesis right through to the first test detonation near Alamogordo, New Mexico."[25]

Maclean was also aware of such pivotal matters as the United States' undisclosed position on emerging international conflicts. During the Korean War, for instance, China and the Soviet Union needed to know whether the United States would pursue the battle into North Korea if China were to send troops into that part of the peninsula to reinforce the Soviet forces already present. Despite its bluster, the private decision of the United States was that it would not follow the conflict into that region. Maclean informed his contacts of this fact, resulting in China, given the green light, abruptly sending in its troops. It is important to note that Maclean, in this treacherous operation, was assisted by Guy Burgess, who used his position in the Department of Far Eastern Affairs to help obtain and convey the classified American information. As we shall see, the men's involvement in this project would ultimately lead to their downfall.

Maclean is also thought to have helped the Iron Curtain descend over Eastern Europe. In 1948, Josef Stalin was fast expanding the Soviet Union's reach while Harry Truman was trying to intimidate him by sending warplanes into Europe said to be loaded with atomic bombs. Maclean sent word to Stalin, however, that the weapons aboard the American aircraft were not nuclear, but conventional explosives, that the United States' show of atomic force was actually a ruse. Stalin, with this critical assurance, continued extending his hold in that part of the world.

Severely stressed by such involvements, Maclean began drinking even more heavily, and, according to friends and colleagues, seemed remote and preoccupied much of the time. He routinely worked until eleven o'clock at night, rarely socialized, and convinced his wife to stay in New York. As its stands, part of his distress may have stemmed from the fact that he was now supplying information to the Soviet Union against his will. It appears the KGB insisted on knowing as much as possible about the American and British nuclear arms programs, but Maclean, who objected to atomic warfare, did not wish to supply the material. He feared it would increase the likelihood of a catastrophic showdown between East and West. So to compel him, the KGB, according to U.S. government sources, assigned Burgess the task of ensuring Maclean's compliance, a project Burgess ap-

proached by hosting a gay sex party and urging the increasingly reluctant operative to attend.[26] Maclean, as expected, did show up at
the gathering, in the course of which he apparently became intoxicated. More important, he became enamored with another man, and
the two soon undressed and had sex. Unknown to either was that Burgess secretly photographed the encounter. Only later did Burgess tell
Maclean about the pictures he had taken of him in flagrante delicto.
Maclean thereafter obeyed all of the Kremlin's demands for atomic
information.

Meanwhile, back in the capitalist world, Maclean was still enshrined as a golden boy in British diplomatic circles, and in 1948 was
once again promoted, this time to Counsellor at the British Embassy
in Cairo. This was a post, however, that he neither sought nor wel-
comed; an understandable reaction considering that Cairo, unlike
Washington, DC, was not a useful KGB venue. Nevertheless, there was
nothing he could do about the assignment if he hoped to maintain his
cover. Feigning pleasure at the promotion, Maclean and his wife traveled to Egypt, where the diplomat became even more agitated and
hostile. Inevitably, he broke down.

It happened when his sister-in-law, Harriet, came to visit. The
Macleans had planned to throw a surprise party for her at the estate of
a Mrs. Tyrell-Martin—"Babsy-Wabsy" to friends—located several
miles up the Nile from Cairo. To make the journey, they rented a
barge and invited eight guests to accompany them. Because of high
winds, however, and because the Nile was beginning to flood, the
two-hour trip became an eight-hour ordeal. Worse, there was no food
onboard, only alcohol, so the high-strung Maclean became roaring
drunk and dangerously angry. When they reached the Tyrell-Martin
property, he grabbed a rifle and swung it wildly at another guest—
a fellow diplomat, for that matter—and broke the man's leg. His out-
bursts did not end there.

In Cairo a few days later, Maclean broke into the home of the
American ambassador's secretary, "dumped her clothes in the lava-
tory, chopped up her furniture and smashed her bath." He did this, he
said, because "the bloody girl's an American."[27] He also trashed his
own house, began pursuing sex with men again, and started calling
himself Gordon, presumably a reference to the well-known gin featuring a wild boar on the label. Maclean then left Cairo.

"He somehow made his way to Alexandria, where he was arrested and placed in a special jail for drunken sailors," it was reported.[28] For the next two days, he did not know his own name.

Exasperated, Melinda Maclean asked her husband's superiors to return him to London for psychological treatment, and they at once complied. As to the reason for his collapse, they attributed it to overwork. A few weeks later in Britain while relaxing and undergoing therapy, Maclean once again became violent, this time in a gentleman's club where he broke glassware and fell to the floor, refusing to leave. His difficulties persisted. Days later, on an elevator that became lodged between floors, he became so utterly distraught that he was finally led weeping from the building. He nonetheless remained firmly rooted in the diplomatic corps, his behavior, as always, being discreetly covered up by the diplomatic community.

At the crest of the Korean War several months later, Maclean was judged fit to return to work and was appointed head of the American Department at the British Foreign Office, a rather astonishing turn of events given his recent history. For the next year, he worked in London during the day, returning home each night to his wife and children in a small, pristine town in the English countryside. What he did not know, however, was that he was now under around-the-clock surveillance for espionage. It seems the Foreign Office was on the verge of concluding that Maclean was one of those who had tipped off the Chinese government about the United States' secret decision not to challenge Communist control over North Korea. Thus, the British government, in the spring of 1951, was quietly, but quickly, constructing a case against him, one that would send him to prison for the rest of his life on a conviction of treason.

EXPOSURE AND ESCAPE

Guy Burgess, on the other hand, never did break down nor did he calm down. During that same season of 1951, he was still drinking profusely and chasing young men at his new location in Washington, DC, just as he had in Britain. But now that he was living in the United States, the risks were graver. The United States was neither impressed with his political connections nor tolerant of his reckless behavior, a reality that hit home when Burgess picked up a hitchhiker, a young Air Force recruit.

The airman, when questioned later by American intelligence sources, told them Burgess had driven him from Virginia to South Carolina. Along the way, he said, they stopped at a roadside motel and had sex, following which Burgess confided in him that he was planning to return to Britain soon in the hope of being transferred to a position in the Soviet Union. Burgess told the serviceman he was tired of "fighting for freedom."[29]

Something else happened on that trip. Three times the men were pulled over for speeding, twice in excess of ninety miles an hour, with Burgess becoming enraged during one of these stops. Insisting on diplomatic immunity, he became belligerent, threatening the officer who stopped him with political repercussions if he tried to make an arrest. The policeman scoffed at the tirade and took the obstreperous statesman before the judge. From there the matter went up the ladder to the Governor of Virginia, who filed a complaint with the British government, a grievance that led to an emergency review of Burgess' job performance. Two weeks later, he was ordered back to London for a meeting with his superiors, a disciplinary conference at which he would be commanded to resign.

Years later, Burgess' old Cambridge chum, Kim Philby, who, as we have noted, had ascended to the status of KGB "master spy" and who was Burgess' senior in the underground Soviet network in Washington, DC, said there may have been a more pressing reason for Burgess' abrupt recall. It seems the FBI, at the same time as the speeding violation in Virginia, informed Philby and other key British officials that it was investigating Burgess on suspicion of espionage; particularly, the role he may have played in supplying China with top secret American information regarding its plans in the Korean conflict. Of course, Philby alerted Burgess to the inquiry at once. This would suggest, then, that the British government may have ordered Burgess to return to London not because of his unprofessional conduct in Virginia but because it feared he might be a Communist operative. Supporting this view is the fact that only a year earlier British intelligence sources had themselves raised concerns about his loyalty, although, presumably out of a sense of national pride, they did not share their doubts with their American counterparts at the time.

In any event, Burgess left for London on the *Queen Mary* in May 1951. As was his way, he met on the voyage an American medical student whom he found charming. So enchanted was he, in fact, that he invited the young man to accompany him on a trip to France the following weekend, and the American agreed. Upon their arrival in London, Burgess reserved a cabin for two on the steamer, *Falaise,* for what was to be a Friday night excursion. Soon after making the reservation, he received a phone call.

According to his long-time housemate, the call completely unnerved Burgess. After hanging up, he hurriedly explained that Maclean was in some sort of trouble and that he had to go to him at once and help him. He then rushed out of the house, never to be seen again by the housemate.

Apparently, Donald Maclean, like Burgess, had learned that his cover was compromised, that the British government was fast becoming aware of the aid he had given the Chinese in the early years of the Korean War. Not only was Maclean alarmed: the Kremlin was worried too, concerned that the unstable operative might crack under British interrogation and reveal Soviet secrets. For this reason, the KGB instructed him to flee to Moscow and enlist Burgess' help in getting there. Burgess was not to accompany him, but was merely to assist Maclean in leaving Britain.

Burgess, however, had other ideas. Facing a forced resignation from the diplomatic corps, and, worse still, being the target of an American probe for espionage, his mental state, according to a friend, was rapidly deteriorating. Having little to lose, Burgess decided to bolt with Maclean. After all, he already had in his possession two tickets on a ship leaving for France that same night.

With this scheme in mind, Burgess drove to Maclean's country house, where he was introduced to Melinda Maclean as "Ronald Styles." After an outwardly normal dinner, Maclean left the house momentarily, supposedly to stoke the furnace, while Burgess chatted with Melinda. Upon returning, Maclean packed an overnight bag and collected his briefcase, then told his wife that he and Burgess were leaving to visit a friend. They would return, he said, the next day. Maclean's two children then came running into the room to tell their father goodbye.

"Get back into bed, you little scamp," he said to one of them affectionately. "I'm not going far. I'll be back soon."[30]

And with that, the two men drove to the south coast of England, boarded the midnight steamer to Saint-Malo, and vanished from the European continent.

Meanwhile, Anthony Blunt, Burgess' old Cambridge friend, fellow spy, and occasional lover, hurried to Burgess' flat in London and disposed of all the incriminating papers he could find. These included handwritten documents and telegrams from fellow Ring of Five operatives John Cairncross and Kim Philby, as well as several love letters implicating Blunt himself. This way, there would be no evidence of any of the men's affiliation with the KGB, nor proof of Blunt and Burgess's own intimate relationship.

The Manhunt

The following Monday, when neither man reported to work, British authorities became alarmed. They did not, however, convey their worries to American intelligence agencies, nor, for that matter, did they notify the press. Instead, they kept the disappearance secret for nearly two weeks, valuable time that, had Western nations been aware of the situation, might have been better used to nab the two agents before they reached sanctuary behind the Iron Curtain. As it turns out, part of the reason for the delay appears to have been related to Prime Minister Winston Churchill's own lack of concern about the disappearance.

According to his personal secretary, Sir John Colville, Churchill did not take Burgess and Maclean seriously. "He merely wrote them off as being decadent young men, corrupted by drink and homosexuality," Colville said.[31]

Many others in the British government were deeply disturbed by the disappearance. On the morning of June 7, the Foreign Office issued the following statement:

> Two members of the Foreign Service have been missing from their homes since 25th May. One is Mr D. D. Maclean, the other Mr G. F. de M. Burgess. All possible inquiries are being made. It is known that they went to France a few days ago. Mr Maclean had a nervous breakdown a year ago owing to overstrain, but was believed to have fully recovered. Owing to their being absent without leave, both have been suspended with effect from 1st June.[32]

Of course, the United States was infuriated by Britain's initial silence on the matter. As for the press, when the Foreign Office statement was released, the strange disappearance immediately received front page coverage around the world.

"Commons Asked to Keep Cool About Two Missing Diplomats," said *The Washington Post,* a newspaper that followed the case particularly closely.[33]

A manhunt was now staged across Europe, and it was a massive one. "Estimates here have more than 25,000 on the lookout for the missing men," wrote Seymour Freidin, Paris correspondent for the *New York Post.*[34]

Searches were conducted aboard Russian cargo ships, in the hill towns of Italy, and especially in the city of Paris, where gendarmes combed the tawdry Pigalle district and interrogated patrons of the smoky cabarets and bohemian cafés of the Left Bank. These latter establishments, said to be frequented by artists, anarchists, and other assorted individualists, were considered likely possibilities because Donald Maclean had delighted in them while a young diplomat in the city. For that matter, it was believed that either man might be drawn to them now, café society being known for its artistic, political, and sexual nonconformity. This included a warm reception for gay men. As one newspaper put it, rather coyly, it was the kind of place "where men make friends easily"[35]; yet the Left Bank, like the rest of Europe, did not deliver the spies. Indeed, the year-long search, said to be "one of the greatest manhunts in European history," proved to be futile, having been launched, as it was, so late after the fact.[36]

As for what actually happened to Burgess and Maclean, a reconstruction of events reveals that they disembarked at Saint-Malo, then, the next morning, took a taxi to a town sixty miles away. According to the driver, they did not speak to each other during the trip. A few hours later, they hopped a train to Paris, then to Geneva, and from there flew to Prague, then Stockholm, and finally Moscow. On the same day that the Foreign Office issued its statement two weeks later, telegrams were received by the men's families, supposedly from the men themselves.

Burgess's was sent from Rome and addressed to his mother. "Terribly sorry for my silence," it read. "Am embarking on a long Mediterranean holiday. Do forgive."[37]

Maclean's telegrams, on the other hand, were sent from Paris. "Am quite all right," said the one sent to his mother. "Don't worry. Love to all." To his wife, he wired, "Had to leave unexpectedly. Terribly sorry. Am quite well now. Don't worry darling. I love you. Please don't stop loving me."[38]

A subsequent investigation revealed the original messages had been sent by third parties, although presumably at the men's behest. Naturally, rumors abounded.

Once the existence of the telegrams became known, kidnapping and assassination were ruled out as possible reasons behind the disappearance. It was now assumed the men were, indeed, KGB agents. Complicating the picture was the fact that they were also gay. It seems British and American intelligence agencies, as well as the public, were convinced a connection must exist between the men's sexual orientations and their treasonous political activities.

"There have been hints that the case is one involving sexual perversion," said *The Washington Star,* implying that Burgess and Maclean, as gay communists—or "red poofters" as they were called in Britain—were lovers who ran off together to the USSR.[39] In another edition, the same newspaper wondered whether "blackmail by Communists was involved in the mystery."[40] And London's *Daily Mail* got into the act. "It is a distasteful subject," it said, "but it is important to an understanding of Maclean's loyalty to the Communist cause to mention that he was also, if intermittently, a homosexual."[41]

Predictably perhaps, next came the accusation that the British Foreign Office itself was a veritable hotbed of homoerotic activity, which elicited howls of protest from within the agency. The Foreign Secretary, among others, railed against the charge that "widespread sexual perversion" existed in the Foreign Office, calling the allegation reckless and unwarranted. Such accusations persisted nonetheless, as did suspicions of extortion.

In reality, it may never be known the degree to which the KGB threatened to expose Burgess or Maclean's same-sex activities. While homosexual blackmail was apparently used at least once against Maclean, it was probably never used against Burgess, a man who was forthrightly, even defiantly, gay since his Cambridge years. Nevertheless, the men's sexual orientations in concert with their traitorous actions—not to mention Britain's lengthy delay in alerting the United States to their defection—carried damaging repercussions for decades to come. According to journalist and CNN commentator Martin Walker, the incident "cast a long shadow over the intimacy and trust between British and American intelligence operations which had been forged in the war against Hitler, and continued throughout the Cold War."[42] The scandal intruded, as well, into the lives of ordinary law-abiding gays and lesbians, saddling thousands of them with social, political, and legal difficulties.

IMPACT ON THE GAY AND LESBIAN CITIZENRY

In both nations, one immediate consequence of Burgess's and Maclean's flight to the USSR was a heightened mistrust of homosexual citizens in general. Whereas there had been, since the beginning of the Cold War, an unfounded suspicion of the gay population's respect for the democratic model, the scandal was taken as confirmation that such dark misgivings had indeed been warranted.

In Britain, this distrust could be seen by the way in which the authorities began treating those with same-sex orientations. Increasingly, conservative members of Parliament took to depicting gays and lesbians as threats to society, with no less a figure than the Home Secretary himself, Sir David Maxwell-Fyfe, delivering a slanderous blow before the House of Commons. In his public tongue-lashing, he accused gay people of being "exhibitionists and proselytizers and a danger to others, especially the young," an aggressively homophobic viewpoint that, within a matter of months, came to be widely embraced by those in the government, as well as by those in law enforcement.[43] "The antigay hysteria of the McCarthy period," says historian Neil Miller, "met the traditional harshness of British law," and the consequences were dreadful.[44]

In England and Wales, for instance, the number of arrests of gay men climbed by over 50 percent between 1950 and 1955, largely as a result of sting operations targeting men seeking consensual sex.[45] Furthermore, those collared in such setups included prominent men, including politicians, journalists, and actors, most notably the gifted thespian John Gielgud, who, upon being released, was told to get psychiatric treatment. Thus, the gay population, while not officially classified as an enemy of the state, came to be perceived and treated as a disturbed and potentially subversive lot, thanks in no small measure to the actions of Guy Burgess and Donald Maclean. As for why gay citizens were assumed to be prone to abetting Communists in the first place, two broad arguments were offered to explain their purported susceptibility.

The first held that a person who has sex with someone of the same gender is, without fail, emotionally unstable, as well as immoral. Accordingly, such an unpredictable and unscrupulous individual would probably do just about anything if asked or paid, and this included spying for the Soviet Union.

The second argument, a far less judgmental one, was legalistic and concerned gay men only, since it was men, not women, whom British law prohibited from having sex with one another. Its premise was that male-to-male relations, being illegal, rendered such men vulnerable to blackmail. By holding sensitive government posts, they were said to be susceptible to coercion by the Soviet Union since, if they failed to comply with KGB demands, their illicit sexual activities could be made public and their lives, as well as those of their loved ones, ruined. They could even face jail terms depending on the information the KGB decided to release.

As for the soundness of these arguments, the first one had no merit whatsoever, while the second possessed little, if any, truth. Given what we know today about the frequency of KGB-ordered homosexual blackmail during that era, it appears that its extent was quite small, no more widespread and probably less prevalent than that involving heterosexual adultery and other socially unacceptable activities or conditions. The fact is, simply no evidence supports the notion that the gay citizenry, fearing exposure, was any more likely than the straight population to be manipulated into spying for the Soviet Union. That said, it should be noted that in exceptional instances homosexual blackmail did occur among some of the operatives themselves, as when Guy Burgess threatened Donald Maclean with compromising sexual photographs. Being a gay spy, then, rather than merely being a gay citizen, could, under extenuating circumstances, make one prone to extortion. Again, heterosexual infidelity and other such acts could also render an operative vulnerable to coercion. In the wake of the Burgess-Maclean scandal, however, it was homosexuality that came to be regarded as a grave threat to national security in Britain and the United States. It was for this reason that London's *Sunday Dispatch,* in direct response to Burgess and Maclean's disappearing act, called upon the British government to follow America's lead in "weeding out sexual and political perverts"; a request that was quickly taken to heart.[46]

Soon after the editorial hit the newsstands, FBI officials arrived in London to confer with representatives of Scotland Yard in an effort to emphasize the dangers posed by gay residents and to help the British beef up their surveillance and incarceration of the homosexual population. Furthermore, the United States, in the ensuing months, continued pressuring Britain to intimidate and suppress the gay citizenry and was largely successful in achieving its aim. This is because Britain, crestfallen by the Burgess-Maclean flap, was eager to atone for its laxity in order to restore its ally's trust. Unfortunately, gay men were finding it much harder to maintain employment in Britain, especially in government posts.

In this regard, a 1952 article in the *Sydney Sunday Telegraph* reported that the British intelligence service, "after the disappearance of Guy Burgess and Donald Maclean, who were known to have pervert associations," had proceeded to compile "a 'Black Book' of known perverts in influential Government jobs." It added, "Now comes the difficult task of side-tracking these men into less important jobs—or of putting them behind bars."[47]

In the United States, this brand of prejudicial treatment was actually formalized, as the federal government flatly refused to hire gay men and terminated those who were already employed. Not that lesbians were exempt from discrimination: during McCarthy's reign, a special committee created to examine the purported link between homosexuality and communism warned of a secret Soviet plot to draw "women employees of the State Department under their control by enticing them into a life of Lesbianism."[48] Of course, there was not a scintilla of evidence to support this outlandish claim, but it was accepted as true just the same, and resulted in countless women blocked from federal employment. The British and American governments were both very forthright about their actions, even boasting publicly of having turned away hundreds of workers due to their purported "moral weaknesses." Naturally, in debates about the matter, the names of Guy Burgess and Donald Maclean would arise as examples of the damage homosexual citizens were capable of inflicting upon a free and unsuspecting people. In this way, the scandal contributed to continued discrimination against gay men and lesbians in employment.

In addition, the Burgess-Maclean affair, as we have seen, contributed to a steep rise in the number of gay men arrested in Britain for consensual sex. Among those whose character was above reproach, yet who nonetheless came to be destroyed by the government's frenzied antigay crusade, was mathematician Alan Turing. A celebrated British patriot, Turing, only a few years earlier, had accomplished the impossible: he had deciphered the secret code used by the Nazis in their submarine warfare, thereby giving Britain and its allies control over the Atlantic during World War II. In 1952, however, during Britain's antigay witch-hunt, the government pressured the shy Turing into conceding that he was gay, then immediately classified him a security risk. He was then coerced into undergoing an experimental hormonal treatment intended to change him into a heterosexual, which succeeded only in causing him physical deformities. Two years later, humiliated and broken, the national hero ate an apple laced with cyanide.

Sadly, Turing's ordeal was not the only one inflicted on a gay citizen by an ungrateful, misinformed government. Other disturbing cases occurred as well, along with a mounting number of reports of police corruption, and these odious incidents did not go unnoticed. The British citizenry, by this time, was becoming suspicious of Scotland Yard, whose officers had taken to tampering with evidence to guarantee convictions of gay men. By all accounts, the antigay crackdown had spun out of control, the authorities obsessed with intimidating and apprehending gay men and ensuring their prosecution at any cost. For this reason, the public took a stand in 1954, the year Alan Turing killed himself. Rankled by the manner in which the police were conducting themselves, the people insisted on a review of police methods. They further demanded that Parliament revisit the nation's law criminalizing consensual sex between men, in an effort to revise or rescind the legislation.

For its part, the government appeared to be responsive to the public outcry, at least superficially. To appease the annoyed public, Parliament appointed a special committee to examine the soundness of the law. A group was formed composed of male and female attorneys, physicians, clergy, and Members of Parliament to assess "the law and practice relating to homosexual offences and the treatment of persons convicted of such offences by the courts."[49] For the next two years, the appointees, as directed, pored over the existing scientific information about same-sex relations, and summoned testimony on sixty-two different occasions from over 200 individuals and organizations, groups that ranged from the Public Morality Council to the Progressive League. Finally, in 1957, the committee wrapped up its study and issued its conclusions.

"Homosexual behavior between consenting adults in private should no longer be a criminal offence," the group said. "Questions relating to 'consent' and 'in private' . . . (should) be decided by the same criteria as apply in the case of heterosexual acts between adults."[50]

Of course, Parliament was dumbfounded by these conclusions, not to mention indignant and unyielding. Bristling at the panel's recommendations, the House of Commons flatly refused to act on them. Instead, it would be another ten years—a decade during which several notable events would increase the visibility and acceptability of Britain's gay citizenry—before the government would at last adopt the committee's advice and strike the destructive law from the books. Nevertheless, in so doing Parliament helped bring the country into the modern age in regard to same-sex love. Consequently, if blackmail had ever been a genuine threat to gay British men during the early years of the Cold War, this legal reform, by placing their sexual behavior well within the law, would help protect them from such dangers in the times ahead. In this way, the law's repeal furnished gay men, as well as the nation itself, with a more secure future.

POSTSCRIPT

As for the Ring of Five's future, its members came to very different ends. The group's most successful operative, Kim Philby, fled to Moscow in 1963 because his cover had been blown and the authorities were in fast pursuit. Once in the USSR, he seduced and married Melinda Maclean, who had moved there several years earlier to be with her husband. Philby also wrote a memoir, *My Silent War,* intended to clarify his values and vindicate his actions as a spy. He then lived out his remaining time in Moscow, with the Soviet government giving him a patriot's funeral with high honors upon his demise. "He died happy, fulfilled, and unwracked by guilt—his final coup," wrote a journalist who interviewed Philby shortly before his death.[51]

In terms of the remaining members, after Philby's defection British authorities unmasked Anthony Blunt, who had become the nation's chief curator of art, or the "Surveyour of the King's Pictures" as his position was officially known. He had also become the lover of Jack Hewit, Guy Burgess's former partner. Although Blunt was granted immunity from prosecution, he was nonetheless stripped of his knighthood and fired from Cambridge. Embittered, he, in turn, informed on John Cairncross, who was now living in the south of France with a young American wife and a dog named Blackmail.[52]

Guy Burgess, for his part, stayed in the USSR, although not entirely of his own accord. In the early 1960s, he asked the British government to guarantee him "safe conduct" home so he could visit his mother—a rather audacious request under the circumstances—but was told he would be arrested if he set foot on British soil. Moreover, after petitioning Britain for this courtesy, he learned that the Soviet Union had already decided to prevent him from going even if Britain agreed to have him. This is because the Soviets were concerned that Burgess, who had now begun showing the signs of advanced alcoholism, might reveal state secrets if interrogated by British intelligence agencies upon his arrival. Thus, he remained in Moscow with his new lover Tolya, a blond electrician, and a job at the State Publishing House compliments of the Soviet government.

"They look after eggheads here," he crowed to a reporter at the time.[53] Indeed, the Soviet government does appear to have tried to make his life a comfortable one. Despite its best efforts, though, Burgess was never truly content in the USSR, where he continued wearing his Eton tie and refused to learn the Russian language. It seems he was homesick much of the time and drank more heavily than ever, usually a fine Georgian wine. He was also known for stopping the rare British or American visitor on the street in an effort to engage the person in conversation just so he could hear his native tongue.

Furthermore, the troublesome, antisocial behavior for which Burgess had become known in the West persisted in the East. At a gala at the Chinese Embassy in Moscow, for instance, he urinated in the fireplace to the astonishment of onlookers, including Donald Maclean, who was mortified by the display.

In one area, however, Burgess adjusted quite well, namely, to his job at the State Publishing House, where he took pride in having arranged for the works of his favorite author, E. M. Forster, to be translated into Russian, along with the books of another writer he admired, Graham Greene. But his publishing career proved to be a fleeting one; the former operative died in 1963 of acute liver failure.

As for Donald Maclean, after arriving in the USSR he made it a point to distance himself from Guy Burgess, although he did agree to deliver the eulogy at Burgess's funeral. Likewise, he kept away from Western journalists, desiring no contact whatsoever with the British or American media.

"I have nothing against you personally," he once told a *Washington Post* reporter who showed up unbidden at his door, "but I just don't want to talk to anyone."[54]

But Maclean certainly did talk to the Soviets. It seems the Soviet government assigned him to the nation's premier think tank, the prestigious Institute of World Economy and International Relations, where he wrote several influential papers and a highly regarded book. Yet after living in the USSR for many years, Maclean became disillusioned with communism, at least with the way it was being practiced in that nation. He felt it was becoming fossilized, as well as self-serving to those in power, and he was especially perturbed by the government's growing disregard for the welfare of the people. Accordingly, he began vocally opposing the Soviet system. He also took a strong stand against the USSR's participation in the nuclear arms race, and became increasingly critical of the oppressive manner in which the Communist authorities were treating citizens who voiced their concerns about the state. Among other actions, Maclean formally complained to Party officials about their heavy-handed, despotic tactics, a risky venture at that time and place. But such acts became typical of him. For the rest of his life, he continued defending political dissidents ranging from historians to physicists, whom the government attempted to force into silence by confining to mental institutions for their unauthorized beliefs.

"Indifferent to considerations of expediency," his colleagues would later write, "and ignoring the threat of personal difficulties, Donald Maclean was guided by his understanding of moral and political duty to take a principled stand in these cases, as in others."[55] Despite all he had experienced, however, he remained a staunch communist, even into his senior years, disappointed with the ideology's application in the USSR but ever hopeful of its prospects elsewhere.

Ultimately, Maclean's most meaningful contribution to Soviet society, in the opinion of charitable historians, was his work at the think tank. There, in collaboration with scores of articulate and determined men and women, he helped in a modest way to usher in the era of perestroika. As fate would have it, though, he was not to witness its actual arrival due to his death by cancer in 1983. As for his final resting place, Maclean was cremated in Moscow. His ashes, as he had requested, were flown back to Britain and placed in his family's vault in the town where he was born.

Chapter 5

An Arrest for Homicide: Simon Nkoli and the Delmas Treason Trial

In 1977, on his twentieth birthday, Simon Nkoli took his lover home to meet the family. A black man born into a South Africa steeped in racism and homophobia, Nkoli did not wish to hide this relationship that meant so much to him. He found it difficult enough coping with the racial prejudice that surrounded him, let alone having to conceal something as essential as his gayness, especially from his loved ones. This, however, is precisely what he had been doing for quite some time, all the while dodging his mother's questions about his personal life. So Nkoli, on this special day, decided to take his partner André, a warm, prosperous white man, to the family home. The occasion proved to be an unforgettable one.

"I can't believe this is happening to me!" Nkoli's mother railed upon meeting the couple. "What is my sin?"[1]

She reminded her son that the family had just recovered from his controversial actions as a student protester; Nkoli had been arrested on three occasions for opposing the government's racist policies. Now his scandalous reputation would be renewed if he were to become known as a gay man involved in an interracial relationship.

Not everyone in Nkoli's family reacted as harshly as his mother. His stepfather, for one, accepted the news much more readily. A chef at a hotel, he tried to reassure his wife by telling her that he had met many upstanding, successful gay people through his job. She should not feel so distraught, he said. Unfortunately, his words only fueled her rage. With no justification, she accused him of being gay himself and forbade him to have close contact with their son. Within days, she also began dragging Nkoli to folk healers, known as *sangomas,* in an effort to rid him of his same-sex desires. Like many people in South

Africa at that time, she believed homosexuality was a sign of be-witchment, the product of a hex that could be removed by a competent healer.

Accordingly, Nkoli's sexual orientation was studied by four different sangomas, who, as was customary, threw bones into the air and interpreted the patterns in which they landed. Using this method, two of the healers concluded that he was not, in fact, cursed, but was simply a gay man. The third one, however, insisted he was the victim of sorcery. Nkoli disagreed, however, and in short order made his feelings known.

"You're lying," he said to the startled sangoma.[2]

"You see!" the healer exclaimed. "The bad spirit is in you!"[3]

The fourth sangoma likewise claimed that Nkoli was cursed, and further recommended he drink his sister's urine to break the spell.

Eschewing such doubtful remedies, Nkoli's mother mulled over the situation and decided to try a different approach, and so, days later, took her son to a Christian clergyman. A bitter man who quoted from Leviticus and lectured Nkoli about sin, the cleric blamed André for leading Nkoli astray, an accusation based in part on the fact that André was white.

"I believed him even less than the sangomas," Nkoli said of the clergyman.[4]

Finally, Nkoli's mother, after talking to André's mother, decided to send both young men, jointly, to a psychologist. Given her traditional views, seeking help from a professional therapist meant she was surely at wit's end. But even the psychologist did not deliver the result she so keenly desired. After extensive psychological workups and several meetings with Nkoli and André, the therapist informed the two men that they were irrefutably homosexual. In addition, he said they were obviously in love and suggested they move in together, advising them that, should they encounter problems because of their races, pretend Nkoli was the household servant. Then, to celebrate their relationship, the psychologist uncorked a bottle of champagne, while announcing that he, too, was homosexual.

Of course, Nkoli's mother was none too happy about this turn of events. "Everyone's gay!" she shrieked when she found out about the therapist, her husband laughing at her bewilderment.[5] Such was the rather farcical coming out of Simon Nkoli, the man who would go on to become South Africa's most persuasive, and heroic, gay figure of the twentieth century.

RACISM AND HOMOPHOBIA
IN SOUTH AFRICA

Nkoli was born in 1957, at a time when South Africa's black majority was launching its grassroots campaign to challenge the white minority's ironclad control over the nation. White people of European descent had ruled the territory since 1652, an oppressive state of affairs that began when settlers representing the Dutch East India Company, a powerful trading firm based in the Netherlands, arrived in the region and set about confiscating land. To hasten this colonization, the Dutch soon began permitting German and French citizens to settle in the region, and, a few years later, those hailing from England, Ireland, and Scotland also began to settle there. In this way, nearly all of South Africa's usable land ended up in white hands. These new immigrants, as well as their descendants, wasted no time exploiting the region's crops, gold deposits, and diamond fields, nor did they hesitate to run roughshod over the territory's indigenous peoples, a situation that worsened after World War II.

In 1948, the white leaders of the Republic of South Africa instituted the infamous policy known as apartheid, a word meaning "separateness" in the Afrikaans language, the hybrid tongue of the Dutch who originally settled there. A scheme of racial subordination, apartheid regarded blacks and other nonwhite groups, namely those of Asian descent and so-called coloreds—people of mixed ancestry—as inferior races.[6] As a result, only white people were allowed to vote, hold government posts, or live in a South African city. The government also enacted legislation to protect the economic interests of the Caucasian race. Certain jobs, for instance, were reserved for whites. Other laws kept blacks and mixed racial groups at a distance from the white citizenry: nonwhite citizens were not permitted to attend schools with white students, were not allowed to live in areas that had white residents, could not use public transportation that was utilized by white people, nor could they participate in sporting events alongside white athletes. Thus, people of color, although they comprised over

85 percent of the population, were treated as nonentities in their own homeland.

All of this began to change, however, in the 1950s, when scores of black, Asian, and "colored" citizens, Nelson Mandela among them, set out to contest the country's racist practices. To this end, they joined the African National Congress (ANC), an organization that protested, through nonviolent rallies, strikes, and boycotts, the government's biased policies. The ruling white government, however, was unsympathetic to the ANC's call for reform. More than that, it was openly hostile to it. Rather than opening a dialogue with the organization, the government tried to silence the group's voice altogether, outlawing the organization and murdering countless of its members in the early years of the antiapartheid movement.

Not only was the nation's racial system prejudicial; its sexual minorities were likewise stigmatized and penalized.

"Apartheid South Africa exhibited a well-developed tradition of legally-sanctioned discrimination against gays and lesbians," writes legal scholar Eric Christiansen. "South Africa had gathered anti-homosexuality laws from each of its several legal traditions—all of which condemned homosexuality."[7]

In this regard, the nation's previous legal systems included the one responsible for authorizing apartheid, and, before that, British common law and the judicial codes of the original Dutch settlers. All of these legislative systems championed heterosexuality, especially its procreative aspect, while criminalizing other forms of physical love, most notably that which occurred between men.

Furthermore, the National Party, which introduced the policy of apartheid in the 1940s, had additional motives for prohibiting homosexuality. For one, it believed there was an urgent need to keep South Africa's white citizenry sexually "pure," so it could better control the nonwhite majority. For another, the party was concerned that the white birthrate was failing to keep up with that of the nonwhite population, a precarious situation given that whites already comprised a minority. For this reason, the South African government encouraged Caucasians to reproduce, while viewing homosexuality as contrary to the long-term social and political interests of the nation's white ruling class.

Because of such concerns, strict new laws were drafted. This new legislation targeted an array of nonprocreative behaviors. The most sweeping of these edicts was the Obscenity Act of 1957, a severe piece of legislation criminalizing everything from homosexual relations to intercourse with "idiots." In spite of such prohibitions, however, relatively few gay people were harassed or arrested when these laws were first enacted, mainly because the gay population, as a whole, was so closeted as to go unnoticed. Trouble began to brew, however, when white gay men, in particular, risked becoming more forthright about their sexual orientations, a gradual process that began in the late 1940s and encountered heated resistance in the 1960s.

Postwar Gay Life in South Africa

Shortly after World War II, white gay men began to discover one another in the urban centers of South Africa. In the port cities, they met at dockside bars—bars that, rather handily, also catered to willing sailors—while in the inland cities they congregated at health clubs, parks, or private parties, or gathered in the cocktail lounges of posh hotels. Except for attractive young seamen, whom everyone seemed to want, white gay men nearly always chose lovers from their own social class, a carryover from the status-conscious heterosexual establishment. Because of this adherence to a timeworn custom, sexual contact between middle-class and lower-class Caucasian men was rather limited.

White lesbians, on the other hand, were not nearly as preoccupied with social standing, and instead appreciated one another more as individuals. Contact among gay women was limited, however, because South Africa, a male-dominated nation, did not allow women as much independence as men, a state of affairs that spilled over into the lesbian community. The problem, says writer Kim Berman, was one of "underexposure, censorship, and patriarchal control."[8] Consequently, the subculture forged by white gay women could not match the organization, influence, and accessibility of the gay male subculture. Still, when lesbians did come together, it most often occurred at coffeehouses, clubs, or private parties, or through groups created by and for female lawyers, nurses, and other professionals.

Black, Asian, and "colored" gays and lesbians had very little contact with the white homosexual community. This was due in part to the sweeping racial segregation that was in place in South Africa during the apartheid era. As noted earlier, existing legislation, by design,

kept the races apart, but this was not the only reason that the races seldom mixed. When nonwhite gays eventually reached a point at which
they could more freely associate with the white homosexual community, the latter shunned their involvement, even when nonwhites sought
to add their voice to the gay rights struggle itself. It was not until the
1980s that blacks in South Africa were finally permitted to play a
meaningful role in gay politics.

As for the activism that existed prior to the 1980s, it was mainly the
product of Caucasian gay men from the middle class, and it was
sparked by a police raid on a social gathering.

It happened in January of 1966. A party with a substantial number
of gay guests, among them lawyers, physicians, and businessmen,
was held in Forest Town, an affluent suburb of Johannesburg. Although the get-together was a peaceful one and took place at a private
estate, the South African police stormed the residence just the same.
What they observed was shocking—to the police, at any rate. Says
the official report,

> There were approximately 300 male persons present who were
> all obviously homosexuals. . . . Males were dancing with males
> to the strains of music, kissing and cuddling each other in the
> most vulgar fashion imaginable.[9]

At once, arrests were made and names were named, and this was
only the beginning. The government set about holding emergency
sessions to ponder the supposedly horrific social event that had taken
place right under its nose, with an eye toward devising new antigay
measures. Predictably, conservatives declared that South Africa was
under assault by the forces of iniquity, the same forces that had led to
the downfall of the Roman Empire. A war must be launched against
the gay citizenry, they argued, and it must be swift and complete.

To this end, several officials decided to get to the bottom of South
Africa's "homosexual problem," so they went undercover to unearth
the chilling truth about the same-sex underworld. When the team
published its findings two years later, though, their report offered no
material of value. Indeed, the scant information they furnished proved
to be superficial at best. Among other insights, the crafty sleuths discovered that white gay men tend to live in tidy, tasteful apartments,
and, among themselves, refer to policemen as "morons."[10] Certainly
there was nothing in their account that was edifying, titillating, or in

any way suggestive of evil agendas or sinister practices. The report made no mention of lesbians or gay people of color, as if they did not exist.

At the same time these lackluster findings were made public, a group of influential white gay men set about systematically lobbying the government to shelve the impending legislation. This pressure proved sufficient to halt the proposed legal action. "Hence, a group of people showed that by mustering their collective efforts, both academically and financially," write Gordon Isaacs and Brian McKendrick, "it was possible to influence significantly the development of public policy."[11]

Although the gay community's efforts were largely effective, the government still modified certain aspects of the Obscenity Act to make it harsher and more far-reaching. Among other amendments, it raised the age of consent from sixteen to nineteen years of age, as well as rendering it illegal for men to display same-sex affection, such as kissing, at social events. The police also cracked down on gay cruising areas and nightclubs, with raids becoming increasingly common. Interracial homosexual contact was also banned, such as it was, a prohibition that did not faze the public given that many whites and nonwhites, gay and straight alike, had long looked askance at mixed relations. For that matter, even heterosexual marriage between the races was illegal.

It was during this time of racial and sexual unrest that Simon Nkoli, in 1977, introduced his white boyfriend, André, to his startled mother and began his visits to the sangomas. Yet as it turned out, Nkoli's mother, to his everlasting pride, came to accept his sexual orientation and eventually championed it. In the ensuing years, the wiry young man also amassed hundreds of active supporters and thousands of admirers around the world for his struggle against the homophobia and racism of his homeland.

The Fight Against Oppression

Nkoli, from the mid-1970s to the early 1980s, was living in South Africa at a time when the nation was spiraling into a social and political abyss. Progressive black leaders, most notably Steve Biko, were urging South Africa's nonwhite people to recognize and respect their own worth on the premise that in so doing they would be able to muster the self-confidence necessary to expel the white minority leadership. In addition, European and North American nations were pressuring the South African government to repeal its racist laws with threats of boycotts, warnings that soon became realities. Further complicating matters was the oil crisis in the Middle East, which was driving up fuel prices and setting off worldwide inflation, with the people of South Africa suffering the effects, especially those in the nonwhite community. Nonwhites whose lives had been hard enough during periods of national prosperity found it even more difficult to eke out a living, a state of affairs that intensified their animosity toward the white minority leadership.

For these and other reasons, South Africa's people of color began engaging in acts of civil disobedience against the apartheid regime, sometimes collectively and often under the guidance of the banned African National Congress or the United Democratic Front (UDF), an antiapartheid coalition. Simon Nkoli was a member of both organizations. In 1981, he also became a regional secretary of the Congress of South African Students (COSAS), another antiapartheid group. It was at this time, because of his experiences with this latter organization, that he decided to incorporate gay rights into his struggle.

Although Nkoli was, by all accounts, a prominent and productive member of COSAS, trouble arose when the organization asked him to bring a girlfriend to its meetings, to which he replied that he did not have a girlfriend, but a boyfriend. At once, the group's leaders expressed their alarm that a homosexual man was holding an important position in the organization and promptly scheduled a series of discussions to determine if he should step down. It looked as if the civil rights group, oddly enough, might be biased against gay people. After days of deliberation, the issue was taken before the entire membership, and 80 percent voted that he should remain in his post. Even so, a handful of COSAS members thereafter taunted him at meetings and discounted his political opinions. Thus, while the incident had been a victory for him in that the organization had ultimately stood by him, it also became a wake-up call.

The following year, Nkoli joined the newly established Gay Association of South Africa (GASA), an organization composed almost exclusively of middle-class white men. He soon found himself disillusioned with this group, too. GASA, he discovered, had no intention of addressing, let alone opposing, the government's policy of apartheid, or any other controversial issue for that matter, because it considered itself a nonpolitical organization. Also disappointing was the fact that the group held many of its meetings in all-white venues such as segregated gay bars, a practice causing Nkoli, one of its only black members, to realize that racism was not confined to heterosexuals. He was not alone in detecting racial prejudice in his white GASA colleagues. Most gay men of color avoided the organization altogether because they did not feel welcome in it.

"Blacks were uncomfortable with GASA from the word go," Nkoli later said.[12]

Despite his unease, however, Nkoli remained in the group with an eye toward upgrading it, and, to that end, succeeded in convincing GASA to stop holding its meetings in segregated settings. He further obtained its white members' pledge to avoid, in their everyday lives, any other sites that refused to allow nonwhites on their premises. Even with these concessions, he still found the organization racist in other respects, and so two years later he formed the "Saturday Group," a GASA adjunct for black gay men. Within months, however, Nkoli's involvement with this new project ground to a halt as South Africa became consumed in rage, as the situation among the races reached a state of undeclared civil war.

Nonwhites rose up against the Caucasian regime, often violently and in response to the government's preemptive strikes against people of color. Panicked, the white authorities, aware they could no longer control the masses through threats and dubious legal maneuvers, hastily imposed media blackouts, bombed the meeting sites of nonwhite organizations, and assassinated key figures in the antiapartheid movement. They also used terror tactics to intimidate ordinary citizens who dared to express their disagreement with South Africa's white leadership.

A mayor of one of the black townships, for instance, testified before the Truth and Reconciliation Commission, a human rights board formed several years later, that the police had repeatedly tried to kill him because he belonged to a prominent antiapartheid organization.

"I had to take precautions about my life," he said.[13] Among other acts, the police bombed his house, shot his dogs, and beat his brother to death, or so they thought. At the mortuary, it was discovered that he was still breathing. The police also arrested the mayor himself, kicked and clubbed him, then tortured him using the "straitjacket" technique, an agonizing procedure in which a plastic bag is placed over the head and face. Such incidents, sadly enough, were not isolated; they had become the order of the day.

Finally, the government, out of sheer desperation, declared a state of emergency and concocted new legislation handing the police near total freedom in treating the nonwhite citizenry however they saw fit. Of course, such laws were unnecessary since existing legislation was sufficient to cover most any criminal act that might occur under an array of circumstances, emergency or otherwise. The truth is, the new laws were designed simply to give government agents a free hand in silencing the nonwhite population on the pretext of maintaining the social order.

Nicholas Haysom, writing at that time, explained that the emergency legislation's unethical nature "is manifest in the provisions which exclude lawyers from access to detainees; it is manifest in the provision which grants policemen wide powers to act on instinct or in error; it is manifest in the indemnity clause which protects the security forces from the consequences of their criminal or unlawful actions."[14] In short, the legislation set loose the police without oversight or accountability during a critical period of civil unrest.

By assaulting civil rights advocates and their organizations for legitimately expressing their beliefs, the government undermined its own reputation. One hard-hitting consequence of this was that corporations around the globe began removing their businesses from South Africa, hence wounding its economy. The white government, its obstinacy entrenched, continued brutalizing the nonwhite citizenry, even going so far as to bankroll vigilante groups, white supremacist squads that raided and torched entire towns of nonwhite men, women, and children. Such was the explosive situation when Simon Nkoli attended a funeral in September 1984, where he was promptly arrested.

THE DELMAS TREASON TRIAL

According to the charges against him, Nkoli had taken part in an antiapartheid demonstration earlier that month during which he threw a rock that killed a man. Nkoli in fact did attend a strike called to protest a discriminatory rental practice and did speak out in support of the cause, but he did not kill anyone; the allegation against him was fabricated. Regardless, the government pressed ahead with its accusation of homicide, as well as treason, locking him away for sixteen months without bail, without access to a lawyer, and no trial date. Furthermore, his situation did not improve anytime soon. The interrogations to which he was subjected were grueling, and focused not only on his politics but on his sex life as well. He was asked such pointed questions as, "Why do you like fucking white men?" and "Why don't you have sex with your own people?"[15] To be sure, being black, gay, and a partner of a white man placed him at a distinct disadvantage in the South African judicial system.

After the interrogation sessions were over the young activist was placed in solitary confinement at Pretoria Central Prison, a desolate and disorienting experience during which he had only a Bible to read. He remained in isolation for several months until, one day, a prison official arrived and announced that, along with twenty-one other defendants, Nkoli would be standing trial in the town of Delmas.[16] Only then was he allowed to meet the prison's other inmates, among them Nelson Mandela, the future president. He also met his codefendants, men who, like him, had been arrested for participating in the rent-control protest. He also met the two attorneys who had agreed to defend them.

Apparently, none of the other defendants, nor their lawyers, knew Nkoli was homosexual, although they soon found out when another Delmas defendant was discovered writing a love letter to a prisoner not involved in the case. This man's "crime" was quickly relayed to the entire group, and a few of the defendants voiced their outrage that the man was homosexual. One of the more quarrelsome defendants even insisted that he would not agree to stand trial with him, and some of the others concurred on the premise that being associated with a gay man might jeopardize their own chances of winning an acquittal. They were, after all, being tried as a group.

But Nkoli would have none of it. Furious over the whole issue, he abruptly announced to the group that he, too, was homosexual, then awaited their response. Their reactions, it turns out, were decidedly mixed.

"Some of the other trialists were fine about my being gay," he said. "Others weren't."[17] Indeed, although most of them were surprised by his out-of-the-blue declaration, a few were irate.

In the weeks that followed, the men discussed among themselves the possible repercussions of Nkoli's homosexuality on their case and in time reached a rather heartening consensus; he should, in fact, be tried along with the rest of them. The two attorneys had insisted all along that he be a part of the case, even threatening to resign if he was not included. And so it was that all of Nkoli's codefendants, by the time the trial rolled around, were in support of him, and several took genuine pride in him. To a large extent, this was due to his honesty about his gayness and the arguments he made attesting to the legitimacy of same-sex love.

According to one of the defendants, Simon's presence "broadened our vision, helping us to see that society is composed of so many people whose orientations are not the same, and that one must be able to live with it."[18]

The defendants were also impressed by the immense support Nkoli was receiving from outside the prison walls. In their view, such advocacy reflected favorably on all of them, which enhanced their prospects of an acquittal or pardon.

It was certainly true that human rights and gay rights groups around the globe focused their efforts on securing fair and humane treatment for the intrepid activist, and strong support came from the United States and especially from Great Britain and the Netherlands. There was one organization, however, that refused to offer any help whatsoever: the Gay Association of South Africa itself, of which Nkoli was still a member.

"GASA did nothing," he recalled bitterly.[19]

According to a former member of the predominantly white group, a man who depicted Nkoli as "a minor player" in gay politics, GASA chose not to offer the imprisoned activist financial, legal, or even moral support because the organization was not a political one. Besides, the man said, Nkoli had been accused of treason and murder, not homosexuality.[20]

Not surprisingly, the decision by GASA to turn its back on a persecuted gay member, evidently because he was black, was viewed as a travesty by integrated gay rights groups in Europe and North America. Certainly the GASA rebuff sparked quite a scandal, and its reputation was so fouled by its racist conduct that the International Gay and Lesbian Association, of which GASA was a member, expelled the South African group a year later. Of course, this, too, proved to be a controversial act. Regardless, internal conflict within GASA, along with financial difficulties, soon forced the organization to cease operations; few progressive South Africans, gay or straight, lamented its demise.

As for Nkoli, the Delmas Treason Trial, as it came to be known, was scheduled to commence in January of 1986. In the weeks preceding the trial, Nkoli diligently prepared for any questions the prosecutor might ask about his homosexual past. During this same period, Nkoli's codefendants became even more supportive of him. As a matter of fact, when his turn to take the stand neared during the trial itself, Popo Molefe, a codefendant and initially a rather homophobic man, praised the activist and tried to bolster his self-confidence, words of encouragement that touched Nkoli deeply.

Finally, on the stand at the Palace of Justice in Pretoria, Nkoli swore that he had not killed anyone during the confrontation in 1984. He also defended himself against the charge of treason, insisting he had not attended a clandestine meeting during which banned political activities were planned. As for his sexual orientation, it was not mentioned until Nkoli introduced the matter himself.

"I needed to prove that I wasn't at a meeting, and so I told the truth, which was that . . . I had been at a GASA event."[21] Ironically, his homosexuality helped provide the alibi he needed, which caused the charges against him to be dismissed at the trial's conclusion in November 1988.

The verdict addressed each charge against each of the twenty-two defendants, and for this reason took four days to read. On hand to hear it were dignitaries such as Archbishop and Nobel Prize winner Desmond Tutu, himself an unindicted coconspirator in the case. In the end, the judge convicted eleven people on charges ranging from terrorism to intent to overthrow the government, while acquitting eleven others.

Popo Molefe, one of those convicted, said of the white judge, "We didn't expect anything different from this man."[22] He added, however, that the extreme verdict revealed beyond a doubt that the judge was deeply prejudiced.

In this way, the contentious proceedings drew to a close, although the trial's aftershocks continued to be felt across South Africa for years to come as the apartheid scheme finally began to crumble.

THE COLLAPSE OF APARTHEID

The year after the Delmas Treason Trial concluded, a new South African leader, Frederik Willem De Klerk, was elected president, the last under the apartheid policy. For the most part, De Klerk was the last because he set about dismantling the biased system in place and began preparing the nation for its first multiracial election. Within a few months of his election, the verdicts of the convicted Delmas defendants were also reviewed, and the men were set free. In addition, De Klerk permitted the African National Congress to again operate freely within the nation's borders and he released Nelson Mandela from prison. Together, De Klerk and Mandela laid the groundwork for South Africa's first majority rule government, a feat for which they shared the Nobel Peace Prize in 1993.

Simon Nkoli, shortly after his release from prison (he had been detained for more than three years, although innocent) returned to gay activism. Within months he established the nation's first truly racially integrated gay groups, the Gay and Lesbian Organisation of the Witwatersrand (GLOW) and the National Coalition for Gay and Lesbian Equality. His influence, however, extended far beyond these organizations.

In the 1990s, it became evident that Nkoli's ordeal in Pretoria Central Prison had left a lasting impression on his codefendants, some of whom went on to hold key posts in the new multiracial government where they worked to protect the gay citizenry's rights. Patrick Lekota, for instance, a Delmas codefendant and today South Africa's Defense Minister, was among those who helped compose the nation's new constitution, an extraordinary document granting gays, lesbians, bisexuals, and transsexuals equal rights in the public and privates sectors. Moreover, he attributed his support for same-sex rights to Simon Nkoli.

"How could we say that men and women like Simon, who had put their shoulders to the wheel to end apartheid," he said, "how could we say that they should now be discriminated against?"[23]

By all accounts, Nkoli's ongoing prison discussions with the other codefendants, as well as their observations of the way in which he lived his life and fought for his beliefs, had ultimately helped the nation's entire gay and lesbian population.

THE ARRIVAL OF AIDS

Even as Nkoli's diligent efforts as a gay activist were helping build South Africa's gay community, another force, a biological one, had set about undermining this same constituency. Specifically, the AIDS epidemic that had swept across Central Africa, North America, and Europe during the 1980s had found its way to South Africa by the early 1990s, where, among other problems, it rekindled racial strife.

Until that time, AIDS in South Africa was viewed as an infirmity of white gay men. When the syndrome began showing up in the non-white sector, however, several disturbing trends ensued. Among the general public, for instance, racism tinged with homophobia re-emerged, a disturbing turn of events given the distress the nation had just endured as a result of the Delmas trial and other prejudicial ordeals. It seems that AIDS offered an opportunity for biased individuals to return once again to the racism of the recent past. Such negative reactions were not limited to the heterosexual citizenry; problems also arose within the gay community itself.

Many young gay men, for instance, fearful of the stigma attached to the disease, stopped coming out publicly as gay; the unfortunate result of their decision to remain closeted thus hindered the gay community's growth and visibility. Animosity also emerged toward that small number of nonwhite men who had been sexually intimate with white South Africans. They were accused of introducing the syndrome into the nonwhite community. The timing of the epidemic was troublesome as well. Because South Africa's gay community was still in its infancy, it had not yet crafted a political structure capable of reaching outwardly to the government for emergency assistance or inwardly to mobilize the gay population itself. Instead, at the precise moment gays and lesbians were beginning to come together as an influential bloc, AIDS threatened to undercut the community.

Worsening the situation, too, were grave financial concerns. AIDS medications were expensive in South Africa, as they were elsewhere in the world, and nonwhite patients could rarely afford them. Many other health care services were also difficult for gays of color to obtain, were very limited, and very costly.

To be sure, the pandemic was creating havoc for the embryonic homosexual community, so Simon Nkoli, fresh from the Delmas trial, decided to use the skills he had honed as an activist to help address some of the problems. But Nkoli had problems of his own. First and foremost, he discovered that he was HIV positive himself, a status he was able to trace back to his years at Pretoria Central Prison. Although at first he was reluctant to go public with the news—he found it more difficult to reveal that he was HIV infected than to reveal he was gay—he had a change of heart when he realized the benefits such an announcement could bring. It is certainly true that Nkoli's subsequent disclosure did attract media attention to the syndrome's impact on the nation's population, particularly its nonwhite segment.

He did not stop with this announcement, however. After making his antibody status a matter of public record, Nkoli set to work building organizations designed to help those who were infected, such as the Township AIDS Project (TAP) and the Positive African Men's Project (PAMP), both of which were racially integrated and advocated AIDS education and treatment. He also remained an active member of the African National Congress and served on the board of directors of the International Lesbian and Gay Association. During that time, he endured his own illness and used it to publicize several issues related to the larger outbreak. Shortly before he passed away on the eve of World AIDS Day in 1998, he was planning a hunger strike to protest the South African government's inadequate response to the pandemic.

Fittingly, in the weeks following his death, Simon Nkoli was honored around the world. By all accounts, he had worked diligently to end racism in South Africa, while struggling doggedly to improve the lives of gay men and lesbians. He had endeavored to do so by shrewdly making use of scandals in which he had found himself, through which he exposed the flaws that lay in the South African society of his day. Thus, through his positive use of negative circumstances, Nkoli's intelligence, creativity, and compassion were revealed, his accomplishments illustrating the good that can come from controversy when one is astute enough to manage it skillfully.

"Whether from the indignity and scars of apartheid, from ignorance and homophobia, (or) from fear and misunderstanding about HIV/AIDS," said an International Lesbian and Gay Association memorial tribute, "Simon's life celebrated hope, survival and a deep-seated conviction that creating a world without prejudice is a duty and a rite of passage for every human being."[24]

Chapter 6

A Life of Dissent: Reinaldo Arenas and the Cuban Revolution

On a sultry spring morning in 1980, a dozen Cuban citizens crowded into a minibus and crashed it through the gates of the Peruvian Embassy in Havana in a desperate gamble to escape Fidel Castro's iron grip. Although the would-be refugees, in their panic, ran over a guard during the episode, they obtained sanctuary nonetheless because Peruvian officials were sympathetic to their plight.[1] The officials were so understanding, in fact, that a few days later they opened the embassy doors to any other Cubans who wished to flee, resulting in over 10,000 men, women, and their children flooding the complex within a matter of hours, while another 100,000 congregated outside the compound, poised to enter. Of course, the Peruvians were overwhelmed by this massive response, but still tried to help those seeking refuge, that is, until the Castro regime blocked the embassy's water supply and cut off its electricity, leaving Peruvian authorities little choice but to turn away the throng.

The demand for asylum, however, did not let up. Thousands of citizens, miserable under the communist dictatorship, continued clamoring for freedom until their unruliness became worldwide news and a threat to the island's stability. Consequently, Castro, fearing a popular uprising, hurriedly announced he would permit those wishing to emigrate to do so provided they sought sanctuary in the United States, his nemesis to the north. He figured the refugees would regret their decision once they experienced life in America. To expedite their flight, moreover, he arranged for a flotilla of fishing boats, catamarans, and other craft to send them from the Cuban port of Mariel to the south coast of Florida in what soon proved to be an embarrassment to the dictator simply because so many people took him up on the offer.

As for the United States, it was dead set against the scheme and publicized its annoyance through the international news media. Among other warnings, it threatened to impose a $600,000 fine on any boat owner whose vessel was caught taking part in the exodus.

"U. S. Cracks Down on Refugee Boats" read the headline of a *Washington Post* article echoing the government's stern warnings.[2] Despite the saber rattling, there was little the American government could do to stem the tide of refugees without appearing cold-hearted before the world. Cubans, determined to flee, continued pouring into Florida.

Ever the opportunist, Castro next began using the boatlift to force so-called "undesirables" off the island, among them "the riffraff, the prostitutes, the crazy ones," in the words of one of his supporters.[3] Another band of his followers bragged that Cuba was sending its "scum" to the United States and threatened to execute a boat captain who refused to cooperate.

"They said if I didn't take them, they would seize my boat, name it the *Fidel* and put me before a firing squad," the man told reporters. To save his skin, he delivered the outcasts to the Florida Keys in spite of the United States' prohibitions.[4]

"Castro is doing what any pirate would do, basically making them walk the plank," said a State Department spokesperson.[5]

The "scum" consisted of the physically and mentally handicapped, along with a portion of Cuba's hard-core criminal element. Included, too, were countless men and women considered anathema to the image and ideals of the Communist state, most notably political dissidents and gay men and lesbians. In this regard, representatives of American gay rights groups surveyed a substantial share of the 125,000 new arrivals and concluded that up to 20,000 were homosexual. Even this high number may have been an underestimation, a spokesperson conceded, since many refused to acknowledge their same-sex orientations. "They fear the United States will deport them if they do," he said.[6] Nevertheless, the majority were up-front about their gayness, including the renowned writer and political nonconformist Reinaldo Arenas, whom the Castro regime, wholly by accident, forced to leave on the boatlift.

Said one of Arenas's impoverished neighbors, "The police came at 4:30 this morning, they had a clipboard with names, and they shouted his name from the street."[7] Authorities then put the writer on a bus to Mariel harbor and bid him farewell.

It was in this brusque manner that Arenas found himself bound for freedom, elated by the turn of events. As for Castro, the bureaucratic blunder infuriated him because he did not want the world to hear the author's accounts of life on the island, but he could do nothing to prevent it. Arenas was free, which is what he had long desired, an escape from his existence in the totalitarian state, an understandable dream given his experiences there. From the day he was born, Arenas lived under the thumb of tyrants: Fidel Castro with his taste for control, and, before that, Fulgencio Batista with his taste for corruption. Neither had any respect for gay men or lesbians, and instead systematically oppressed or exploited them.

THE BATISTA ERA

An army sergeant whose revolutionary group gained control of Cuba in 1933, Batista's first act was to bestow upon himself the title of General. He then set out to enrich himself by selling off Cuban resources to foreign interests, mainly American ones. He profited for only a short time because the Cuban people became so enraged by his brazen corruption that they abruptly replaced him with a new leader, although unfortunately this was a correction that proved to be short-lived. Bastista, after a brief respite in the United States, returned to the island in the mid-1930s, and with the aid of its military forces overthrew, in 1952, the legitimately elected government. He subsequently ruled the nation until 1959, all the while enjoying the support of the U.S. government. In due course, however, this backing came to a halt as the Cuban people's struggle to eject the dictator began to create such havoc that it jeopardized the island's economy, a precarious state of affairs that caused the United States to decide that Batista had become an obstacle to American interests and should be deposed. To help engineer his downfall, the United States stopped endorsing him. Thus, he threw himself a lavish farewell party at the island's glitziest resort, the Tropicana, then left Cuba and never returned.

Still, before his banishment, the calculating dictator made himself indispensable to the United States. During his stay in power, he tirelessly curried favor with the American government as well as with key figures of the American mafia, Meyer Lansky among them. Among other arrangements, he made a sizable share of the nation's crops, most notably its sugar and coffee, available to powerful U.S. companies, which reaped immense profits from them. By opening the doors to the organized crime syndicate in 1933—the United States was still in the grip of Prohibition—Batista also transformed Cuba into a playground for wealthy and often unscrupulous Americans; its capital city, Havana, brimmed with opulent casinos even as the city streets teemed with destitute Cuban citizens. Although Batista amassed great personal wealth as a result of his manueverings, the Cuban people continued to have little or no access to basic education or health care, and the majority of its citizenry existed in abject poverty.

Gay Sex in the Batista Era

To appreciate Batista's exploitation of the citizenry, we need only look to Cuba's sex industry. To indulge those rich Americans who came to gamble or arrange dubious business deals with underworld figures, Batista's regime made sure that prostitutes were available for their enjoyment. In fact, it has been estimated that as many as 15,000 Cuban women found themselves relegated to prostitution during the 1950s, since few alternatives were open to them.[8] As with the nation's men, Cuban women had to work to support their families, and prostitution was one of the few trades that offered a sufficient income yet did not require an education. Gay male hustlers were easily obtainable as well, many of whom were still in their teens. To prevent foreign visitors from contracting sexually transmitted diseases, Batista required his nation's sex workers to submit to regular checkups. To be sure, guaranteeing the satisfaction of the moneyed Americans flocking to Havana was a top priority of his dictatorship.

"A tourist arriving in Havana was met by a galaxy of 'performing artists' unknown today," writes journalist Todd Anders,

> There were the prostitutes, both male and female, flourishing their licenses, government-issued and carefully administered . . . and there were the hawkers of wares and entertainment. It was not unusual to be approached, at the gangplank, by a young sultry Latin whispering, "Exhibicione! Exhibicione!"[9]

Ian Lumsden, a political scientist at York University, explains that Havana had been renowned for its same-sex prostitution since the 1800s, but that the gay sex trade became even more visible, and more profitable, during the Batista era. "Havana's homosexual cruising areas were well known for over a hundred years," he writes. "Havana's notoriety was similar to that of other port cities such as Marseilles and New Orleans."[10] The city reached its zenith as a sexual paradise in the 1950s when the Batista regime legalized and institutionalized prostitution. This was also a time when the city's tolerant social climate attracted scores of gay men and lesbians from Cuba's outlying provinces—men and women uninvolved in the sex industry—who came to find love, as well as to affiliate socially with others who were homosexual. Indeed, because of the large number of gay people who lived in prerevolutionary Havana, there developed, in the densely populated urban center, a feeling of kinship among many of those with same-sex orientations.

"Perhaps the majority of Cuban gays never experienced what we in the United States call gay community," writes journalist Allen Young. "But homosexuality both visible and invisible was a part of the social fabric."[11]

This is not to imply that gay people moved to Havana only to find romance and a sense of belonging, however. Many relocated so they could live more openly gay lives, while others hoped to forge careers in the arts or letters. Some, of course, planned to do both, such as poet and playwright Virgilio Piñera, who moved to Havana expressly to immerse himself in both sex and art. He remained in the city for the rest of his life, and eventually won acclaim for his verse and plays. Several other gay and lesbian writers and artists also gravitated to Havana, men and women who, in due course, became celebrated for their professional accomplishments.

In other cases, gay Cubans lived in the city since they were born. If they hailed from poor families during the Batista years, often they ended up in the sex trade. If they were lucky enough to have been born into well-to-do families, however, many times they formed enduring same-sex relationships while their relatives simply looked the other way. Such was gay life among the urban elite.

In regions located some distance away from Cuba's cities, on the other hand, homosexuality was viewed rather differently. It was met with *machismo*—the display of excessive masculinity, often associated with sexism—which ruled the day. In several respects, being gay in the countryside was more complicated than being gay in the city, and that included a distinct double standard for women and men. Whereas women in Cuban villages had little opportunity, or sanction, to explore their emotional and sexual desires outside the marriage bed—the woman's place was believed to be in the home—Cuban men enjoyed remarkable sexual freedom that allowed them to indulge in extramarital liaisons, as well as homosexual trysts provided they did not make it known publicly they were engaging in sex with other men.

"Rural Cuba's sexual culture was repressive for women," writes Lumsden, "but it left space for all sorts of sexual adventures between men."

> It allowed homosexuals surreptitiously to conquer supposedly "real" men in private. It even allowed them to flirt with "horny" machos in bars catering to their respective needs, which could be found in many provincial cities. . . . Still, rural values made life hard for males who were publicly identified as homosexuals.[12]

A glimpse into rural gay sexuality during the Batista period can be found in the writings of Reinaldo Arenas, the author whose escape from Cuba was recounted at the beginning of this chapter. In his literary work—compositions that were both lyrical and honest—Arenas portrayed the dilemma of gay men and lesbians living in Cuba under the commands of Fulgencio Batista and Fidel Castro, the latter consisting of blatantly oppressive conditions that Arenas challenged throughout his life, even after fleeing the island.

REINALDO ARENAS

Born illegitimately in the summer of 1943, during the Batista era, Arenas grew up with his mother and her family in the Cuban countryside. The family was so impoverished that it was reduced to living in a shanty with a dirt floor and a thatched roof. Not surprisingly, among Arenas's earliest memories is the sensation of hunger. More disturbing, one of his childhood foods was dirt.

In the home, his grandmother, the matriarch, was a veritable force of nature, a woman who struggled to instill conventional values in her children and grandchildren. Among other things, she sought to teach them respect for the cultural notions of *machismo* and heterosexual love, marriage, and family. These teachings had little effect on young Arenas, who, like many gay people, knew at an early age that he was homosexual. He even remembered the precise moment when he discovered, at the age of six, his attraction to other boys, an epiphany that occurred as he strolled the banks of the Río Lirio where he came upon a group of young men swimming and bathing in the nude. Their nakedness stirred him deeply.

Two years later, Arenas discovered another aspect of sex—intercourse—which he experienced with his male cousin Orlando, who was twelve years old. In his memoir, Arenas explains that their behavior was common in rural Cuba, that most young men in the countryside experimented with homosexuality despite the cultural proscriptions against it.

This was certainly true in the provinces during the Batista era, a period during which the authorities were concerned chiefly with acquiring wealth and power, and had little interest in the day-to-day activities of the citizenry. Perhaps this was a blessing for gays and lesbians. It was preferable, for sure, to the politicization of homosexuality that would develop after Batista was deposed.

Although the dictatorship granted the populace unprecedented sexual freedom, it ruthlessly oppressed the same citizenry in other ways. Furthermore, Batista's minions became increasingly violent as the Cuban people rose up to protest his injustices; infractions that were becoming rampant across the land.

For Arenas, the friction between Batista and the Cuban people became most apparent during the winter of 1957, a season known as "Bloody Christmas." During the holidays, the dictator's henchmen brutally attacked anyone who dared oppose the regime, slaughtering several dissenters on the streets of Arenas's village.

It was because of such barbarism that Arenas decided to join Fidel Castro's revolutionary movement, accompanied by his boyfriend at the time, a youth named Carlos. Their plan was to make their way to a rebel camp in the mountains, and, once there, help overthrow Batista. At the crucial moment, however, Carlos failed to show, and Arenas went alone to the camp where he discovered that its insurgents would not allow him to join in combat because he was merely fourteen years old. He did, however, remain with the rebels and serve as their attendant, and for this reason came to be praised as a young hero after Batista fled Cuba in 1959 and Castro became the nation's new leader. Among other awards, he received a scholarship to a state-operated polytechnic institute where he was told he would study agricultural accounting. What Arenas did not know was that Castro was rapidly establishing another dictatorship, one that would prove even more oppressive than that of Batista and would have as one of its early objectives the confiscation of all of the country's farmland, hence the need for agricultural accountants.

THE CASTRO ERA

The polytechnic institute Arenas attended housed and trained 2,000 students, mostly young men, who were not allowed to leave the premises without authorization. The school was, in reality, a communist indoctrination center. He soon discovered that to obtain his degree in accounting he would be required to take, in addition to the standard business courses, classes in Marxism. He also would be required to climb a towering mountain peak on six separate occasions because, he was told, he was being trained as a soldier, as well as an accountant. Literally overnight, Arenas, like all of the other male students, had been conscripted into Castro's army and was now expected to defend the dictatorship. After graduating, he also would be expected to manage the fiscal affairs of a so-called People's Farm.

In terms of student life, conditions at the school were tense; officials staged political, religious, and moral purges on a regular basis. The strain was so great, in fact, that some of the pupils committed suicide, and over half of those enrolled failed to graduate. Students either quit or were expelled, often for minor infractions, including sexual ones.

The school consisted chiefly of male adolescents, and although the school prided itself on being a macho institution, same-sex desire was in the air. For this reason, gay sex was forbidden. Certainly the consequences of being caught with another student of the same gender were enough to give one pause.

When a gay youth was discovered, for instance, officials would dismiss him immediately, administrative action that would be recorded in his permanent file. This document would then follow him, and work against him, for the rest of his life. The young man would also be ordered to return all of his state issued belongings, a humiliating experience that required him to carry them to the warehouse as the other students threw rocks at him.

This is not to imply, however, that same-sex relations did not occur at the school and on a frequent basis. The fact is, a substantial share of the students had sex with one another, as well as with the staff. Says Arenas,

> One of the professors, if not the majority, had sexual encounters with their students. . . . There was one, Juan, who had relations with close to a hundred students. Sometimes the young men lined up by his room to fuck him; I actually saw this.[13]

On another occasion, Arenas recalled how officials learned, late one night, that several students had jumped over the institute's outer walls. They planned to meet up with a gay man from a nearby town who had agreed to have sex with them. As could be expected, school officials responded at once. They ordered the entire student body to assemble where the officials lectured and threatened all of the students, then made them watch the Soviet propaganda film, *The Life of Lenin*. But this was not the end of it. From that point forward, the student body was required to gather each evening and watch political indoctrination movies. Such overstated methods help account for the school's extraordinary attrition rate.

Cuba, as a nation, was just as oppressive; its homophobia became institutionalized as Castro consolidated his power. For the most part, his regime's antigay stance was a recycling of the same Marxist ideology that had been popular in certain European nations during the nineteenth century and put into action by Josef Stalin in the Soviet Union in the twentieth century. According to Young, in the 1930s one found in the USSR "the exaltation of heterosexuality and the family as ideals for the Soviet citizen," as well as commitment to political revolution itself.[14] The same held true in Cuba during the 1960s. Castro, on more than one occasion, stated unequivocally that those who were homosexual were incapable of becoming true revolutionaries and genuine communists. Due to such narrow views, gay men and lesbians were effectively shut out of the political system.

There was another reason for the government's intolerance. A large-scale effort was being made to transform the nation's image from that of a licentious nation, which it had acquired during the pre-revolutionary era, into a more virtuous one under the new political system. Castro, it seems, associated homosexuality with U.S. mafia-controlled corruption and prostitution, and thus regarded gay males, and to a lesser extent, lesbians, as lingering by-products of the Batista years. For this reason, he instituted a sweeping program to "reeducate"—or, more precisely, to indoctrinate—those said to have been contaminated by his predecessor's decadence.[15]

"At first only the prostitutes were reeducated," says Enrique Raab, a journalist who visited the island during this period. "This caused the leaders to think that homosexuality was also correctable through re-education. There's a great deal of ignorance and a certain amount of machismo among the leaders."[16]

It was certain that virtually any citizen whose sexual style strayed from the norm was considered a potential threat to the regime, and, at a minimum, placed under surveillance. This entailed observation by Castro's police and by neighborhood watch groups composed of zealous communist citizens. In this manner, a Big Brother mentality swept across the island, and gay people were high on the list of suspected nonconformists.

Despite such growing oppression, however, Arenas himself was not yet in danger because his defiant literary work was largely unknown—for that matter, most of it was not yet written—and as a gay man, he was still rather closeted. During his late teenage years, in fact, he was celibate, believing that Castro might be right, that same-sex relations might indeed be unnatural. For a time, the regime's attempts to depict homosexuality in corrosive terms caused him to avoid sex altogether.

Not only was Arenas unsure of the legitimacy of his sexual desires, he was also discontented with his professional life. After graduating from the institute, the regime ordered him to manage the financial affairs of a chicken farm in a rural province, an appointment he despised. Bored on the job, he spent his free time composing poems and short stories, something he had done since he was ten years old. Soon, he also began spending it in bed with a good-looking young man named Raúl, despite his doubts about the normality of same-sex love.

As gratifying as their relationship proved to be, it came to an end a year later when Arenas, desperate for change, transferred to Havana.

To help bring about this move, he requested a trip to the capital city purportedly to help design the accounting curriculum at the University of Havana. Once there, Arenas, like many young men from the provinces, found himself captivated by the city's vibrancy and anonymity, but despite the tempting circumstances did not use the opportunity to explore his sexuality. In part, this was because Castro's troops had begun cracking down on gay men and lesbians and Arenas feared being caught. It was also because he still harbored concerns about his same-sex desires, ambivalent at the prospect of being gay. Many of his colleagues at the university, on the other hand, felt quite at home with their own homoerotic urges, time and again enjoying sex with one another, and with relative abandon. In his chronicle of life in Cuba, Arenas recounts how he often heard these men making love, and describes the intense yearnings their sounds kindled in him. As a result, he increasingly felt the need to break free, both sexually and artistically.

With this in mind, the following year he entered a short story, "The Empty Shoes," in a national literary contest, and the story won. More important, it landed him a job at the National Library, where he was finally able to meet and befriend the nation's top gay authors and embark on a literary career of his own.

Literary Life

Fortunately for Arenas, the library's director was a principled, generous woman who used her position to shield uncompromising authors from Castro's despotism. Among her flock were the renowned gay writers Virgilio Piñera and José Lezama Lima, both of whom opposed the regime's tyranny and whose positions at the library allowed them to continue creating their works. Arenas's job was to locate books requested by patrons, although the director and her resident writers also urged him to read the library's holdings and begin work on the novel he had longed to compose. He did, penning a book titled *Celestino antes del alba* (Singing from the Well).

The novel tells the story of a destitute peasant boy who retreats into his imagination in a desperate effort to cope with reality. In the book, Arenas celebrates the human spirit, while presenting same-sex love as a natural, healthy act. The narrative itself is fluid and the sense of time, fractured, with the story having three separate endings that further distort the sense of reality. By all accounts, the novel was a distinctive entrée by the innovative, twenty-two-year-old writer whose unique voice was quickly recognized and applauded by the literary establishment.

In 1965, *Singing from the Well* received a national award, and, two years later, was published in Cuba. Unfortunately, it would be the only one of Arenas's works to be made available in his homeland. Due to his narrative style, along with his writings' gay content, the book was met with disfavor by the Castro regime, which preferred social realist writings that promulgated classic Communist ideology. In fact, in a short time the government would manipulate the literary creations of all of the nation's writers, going so far as to take control of the National Library itself. In this travesty, Castro accused its director of lesbianism and seditious activities and summarily fired her, then replaced her with his own choice for the job, the nation's loutish chief of police. Appalled by this turn of events, Arenas resigned days later and took a job at the Cuban Book Institute.

While there, he wrote his second novel, *El mundo alucinante* (Hallucinations), later renamed *The Ill-Fated Peregrinations of Fray Servando*. It told the tale of a nineteenth-century Mexican priest who is incarcerated because his sermons are unpopular. As with Arenas's first novel, this one also won a national award but was banned by the regime because it explored the damaging effects of political oppression. When the government announced the book's proscription, it added that Arenas's first novel was henceforth being forbidden along with it.

A cloud of suspicion had suddenly fallen over the writer. Although the authorities did not yet know Arenas was gay, they did know he had expressed concerns, in print, about the adverse impact of totalitarianism and thus was a freethinking man who, in their view, should be monitored and controlled. Even so, this did not stop him from writing.

Although he was now aware that he was under surveillance, Arenas continued submitting poems and short stories to the periodicals of the Cuban Writers and Artists Union. Characteristically, his works revealed his respect for same-sex love, as well as his abhorrence of communism and its devastating effect on the human spirit.

Writes Francisco Soto, a literature professor at the City University of New York,

> Arenas's militancy was in support of individual freedom. If one thing is constantly repeated throughout his work it is the challenging and undermining of all systems of power that attempt to establish themselves as absolute authority. . . . His rebelliousness and subversion were creative and directed toward positive and life-affirming actions: the right of individuals to express themselves freely.[17]

Castro, meanwhile, continued tightening his grip on the gay and lesbian population, his antigay campaign reaching fever pitch by the mid- to late 1960s. Among other acts, his regime created "Yellow Brigades" to prevent effeminate boys from growing into gay men; these were indoctrination units geared toward toughening up such children in the misguided belief that physical endurance would somehow change their sexual orientations. Boys in these squads were forced to wear yellow emblems indicating their so-called problem, femininity, then put to work. Regrettably, for homosexual adults, the situation was even worse.

Beginning in 1965, the government began operating forced-labor facilities—concentration camps—called *Unidades Militaries para el Aumento de La Producción,* 'Military Units for Aid to Production' (UMAP). These centers were created for "antisocial" citizens (shorthand for gay men), although a small number of heterosexual men were also included. Among these men were those who complained about their work assignments, wore their hair long or their pants tight, or donned the psychedelic clothing popular during the 1960s, which was regarded by Communist forces as a sign of Western decadence. The camps imposed backbreaking labor with meager food and rest, their unspoken purpose being either to break the inmates' spirits so they would conform to the regime's demands, or, failing this, to destroy them altogether.

As could be expected, the UMAP facilities were ghastly; so bad, in fact, that some of the prisoners tried to kill themselves. One young villager who watched a truckload of gay men being transported to a worksite described it this way:

Right in front of us on the road was a truckload of UMAP men in their blue uniforms. . . . They were homosexuals. . . . Well, one of those sitting at the back suddenly jumped down and ran past the truck carrying them and threw himself in front of it. He wanted to kill himself. That is how desperate he was. . . . I was one of the ones who took him to the hospital at El Diego de Avila. He was fortunate—he tore up an eyebrow, scraped his face and lost a four-tooth plate. He was out of his mind with desperation![18]

Fortunately, despite the efforts of the Cuban government to conceal the atrocities taking place in the camps, a handful of people, including Arenas, leaked reports to human rights commissions outside Cuba. As a result, the camps drew worldwide condemnation and were closed down four years later. It has been said, however, that they also were discontinued because they were failing to transform homosexual men into heterosexuals, as could have been predicted. In fact, it seems the UMAP facilities may have had the opposite effect. Arenas, for one, believed the regime's campaign to crush homosexuality only served to drive more men toward same-sex relations as a means of defying Castro. Arenas writes,

I think that in Cuba there was never more fucking going on than in those years, the decade of the sixties, which was precisely when all the new laws against homosexuals came into being, when the persecutions started and concentration camps were opened, when the sexual act became taboo.[19]

Arenas, who was a young adult in the 1960s and completely at ease with his gayness, became an enthusiastic player during this sexually-charged season. He says that he was most attracted to macho men who claimed to be heterosexual and served as "tops" for other men. Despite this preference, however, he did not reject the alternative. On those rare occasions when he was unable to find a commanding paramour, he would simply seduce a more submissive man, then serve as the active partner himself. To be sure, Arenas was nothing if not versatile, as well as prolific in his conquests. By his own estimate, he had slept with 5,000 men by the time he was twenty-five years old, a sizable share of whom he picked up at Cuba's lush beaches where eager men were easy to find.

Unfortunately, the intrepid writer also found trouble one day while cruising the beach, an experience that would forever change the course of his life.

PROSECUTION AND PERSECUTION

As Arenas tells it, he and longtime friend Pepe Malas went to a favorite beach one summer afternoon looking for action and soon found it with two handsome and willing young men. Although Arenas does not provide the ages of these partners in his accounts of the ordeal, apparently both were young yet technically not underage, and he was thirty years old. Age not a barrier, the four men gathered in the mangroves and had sex, after which Arenas and Malas left their beach bags on shore and went swimming. When they returned, they discovered that their youthful lovers had made off with their belongings, and so Malas, furious, called the police. At once, the authorities arrived and after a short search found the two youths with the stolen property still in their possession. Despite being caught with the goods, however, in a moment of desperation the culprits insisted that Arenas and Malas had made unwanted sexual advances toward them. They added that this brazenness had offended them and therefore they had chased away Arenas and Malas, who, in their haste, forgot to take their belongings. The young men said they had picked up the beach bags and were planning to return them to the police station.

Of course, their story was ludicrous, but the police arrested Arenas and Malas just the same. In Castro's Cuba, evidence was not required to detain a person for homosexual conduct; merely an accusation was enough. This is how the victims of a petty robbery ended up behind bars themselves awaiting trial for attempting to corrupt two supposed minors.

Shortly after their arrest, Arenas and Malas were bailed out of jail by friends and a trial date was set. Unfortunately for Arenas, though, the authorities subsequently discovered that he was a writer who had smuggled controversial work out of Cuba and was already under the watchful eye of Castro's police. Thus, his arrest for sexual misconduct came to be used as a pretext for pursuing him as a political dissident.

Arenas had smuggled novels out of the country six years earlier when he had the good fortune to meet the renowned painter Jorge Comacho and his wife Margarita, who were on an official visit to Cuba. Comacho had left the country in 1959 and settled in Paris, where he had continued painting, and he maintained a keen interest in the political affairs of his homeland. In 1967, at a time when Castro was attempting to whitewash Cuba's image so as to counter the rush of reports about his regime's abuses, the dictator arranged for an international art exhibit to be staged in Havana. Among other painters, he invited Jorge Comacho to display his work. While the Comachos were attending this event they read Arenas's novel, *Singing from the Well,* then set up a private meeting with him at their hotel to discuss his experiences on the island.

Without hesitation, Arenas told them about the forced-labor camps, the plight of gay men and lesbians, the persecution of political dissidents, and the stifling of artistic freedom. Sympathetic to his plight, the Comachos offered to smuggle his novels to Europe with them— Arenas had completed two by this time—where they would be published. As well, they vowed to stay in touch with him after their departure and continue assisting him from Paris. It was in this way that his books came to be published in France a few months later and to worldwide acclaim. In fact, *Singing from the Well* won France's esteemed Prix Medici for Best Foreign Novel. Although the book impressed the literary world, it annoyed the Castro regime to no end, which caused Arenas to be dragged before the authorities and interrogated about his foreign connections. Predictably, given his ethics, he refused to name his contacts or explain how his manuscripts made their way to France, a lack of compliance that was duly recorded in his file at State Security. If he were found guilty of sexual misconduct at his upcoming trial, the government would be in a position to grill him again, but this time at length because he would be locked up for years, out of public view. Indeed, this eventually is what happened.

Before being imprisoned, Arenas jumped bail and succeeded in dodging the police for four months. During this time, and through the gallant efforts of a former lover, he tried to flee from Cuba on a homemade raft but ended up swimming several miles back to shore, exhausted. Deciding his situation was hopeless, he slashed his wrists, which he thought was better than being apprehended by Castro's police, but did not die, rather, he merely lost consciousness. The next day, weak and disheveled, he made his way back to Havana, where he lived in hiding in Lenin Park during the winter months while the government circulated spurious stories about his being an operative of the Central Intelligence Agency, a rapist who had assaulted an elderly woman, and a homicidal counterrevolutionary, anything to frighten the people so they would notify the authorities if they spotted him in their neighborhoods.

As for his day-to-day existence in the park, Arenas made the most of it given the hardships it entailed. His friends visited him at night and supplied him with food and books, along with paper and pencils so he could continue writing. It was while he was holed up, in fact, that he began composing his autobiography, *Before Night Falls,* a title he devised because he could only write while there was sunlight and because he feared that his life was about to be extinguished. He smuggled a document to Jorge and Margarita Comacho in Europe, too, with instructions for them to publish it as soon as possible. It was an open letter addressed to the United Nations and the International Red Cross that began by explaining that he was being persecuted by the Cuban regime. It proceeded to expose the evils of Castro's Cuba, emphasizing its systematic efforts to crush the nation's writers. Prophetically, Arenas ended with a statement saying that while the content of the letter was true, if the regime were ever to apprehend him it would undoubtedly force him to retract his words. The purpose of the closing statement was to ensure that any future disavowal on his part would be disregarded.

While in Lenin Park, Arenas, lonely and often cold at night, also took hallucinogenic drugs supplied by his friends to help cope with the ordeal. Although the drugs allowed him a brief respite from his troubles, on one occasion they impaired his judgment so badly that the police nabbed him and took him to jail. En route, he again tried to kill himself, this time by swallowing all of the pills in his possession, but he succeeded only in placing himself in a coma. Several days later he awoke in the infirmary of El Morro Castle, a penitentiary near Havana. This time, there would be no escape.

Suffering and Scandal

Thanks to the efforts of the Comachos, Arenas's arrest, his four months on the lam, and his rearrest became a media sensation. Journalists around the world suddenly focused on his dilemma, and nearly all of them decried the hounding of the daring writer. In the words of one European journalist, Arenas had become "a rebel with a *cause célèbre*."[20]

But the Castro regime was not stupid. Because the world cringed when the Cuban government claimed the author had been arrested for having sex in the mangroves, that his political writings had nothing to do with it, the government quickly affixed an array of melodramatic allegations in a clumsy effort to demonize him and thus justify its actions.

For the next several months, and without a trial date, Arenas languished in El Morro prison, where gay inmates were housed in the most run-down section of the facility, segregated from the heterosexual prisoners. In this one respect he was lucky. Although he had been arrested for having sex with men, the charge was eclipsed by the unofficial allegations of murder, rape, sedition, and espionage, such that the authorities, with little forethought, placed him in the prison's non-gay cellblock.

Arenas, although surrounded by willing men, made love only once during his prison term—he pleasured a tall, kind black man in the showers toward the end of his stay. The reason Arenas abstained from sex was because he did not believe two people, regardless of gender, could be emotionally and spiritually free enough to experience sex as it should be experienced while confined against their will. Another reason he abstained was because Castro was known to send agents into El Morro disguised as prisoners in a devious effort to befriend the inmates, then pry information out of them. Aside from Arenas's own decision to eschew intimate relations, a large portion of the inmates were sexually involved with one another, usually without being caught and sent off to the gay sector, a truly horrific place.

Although Arenas, as a rule, did not have sex with other inmates, he did strike up friendships with some of them. When requested by prisoners who were illiterate, he would write touching letters to their loved ones on their behalf. He also stayed in written contact with his own friends and family on the outside. After several months of imprisonment, the government inexplicably brought his mother to visit him. Shortly thereafter, he understood why.

To the foreign press covering the scandal, it was assumed, correctly, that Arenas had been arrested for having sex with two younger men and, for political reasons, was unofficially accused of several unrelated crimes and held at the nation's main prison, El Morro. The media knew he was there because his mother had visited him and vouched for the fact that he was alive and well. It was for this reason that the government had taken her to visit him: to allay the concerns of international human rights groups that were monitoring his incarceration.

The fact is, soon after her visit the Castro regime secretly transported Arenas to State Security headquarters, a lethal center known as Villa Marista. At this facility, political dissidents were beaten, suffocated, and subjected to other agonizing measures designed to force them into divulging their political connections and recanting their previous statements and actions. Abuse was both mental and physical, often resulting in shattered minds and bodies and sometimes death. Arenas was aware that if he were to die at the hands of his tormentors—a distinct possibility—the government's cover story would be that he had been killed by another inmate at El Morro prison, since his transfer to the State Security center was not known by anyone outside of the regime itself.

At Villa Marista, he was placed alone in a closet-sized cell with a gas pipe in the wall through which hot steam could be released to intensify his discomfort. After four days, he was moved to an interrogation chamber where he was drilled mercilessly about his friends and colleagues, with emphasis on his European contacts. Still, despite excruciating sessions that involved beatings, at no point did Arenas reveal the Comachos' names nor finger any Cuban dissidents not already known to Castro's agents.

The scandal surrounding his imprisonment continued to rage, particularly in Europe, with human rights groups insisting the regime reveal his whereabouts. It seems that after the government whisked Arenas away to State Security headquarters, watchdog groups, as well as the foreign press, became suspicious of the silence that suddenly surrounded the case. For this reason, they demanded proof of his well-being, along with information about his place of detention, but the Cuban government was reluctant to produce Arenas himself and had no intention of admitting he was being tortured at State Security. Consequently, Castro's forces, in a rush to return him to El Morro, stepped up their efforts to extract from Arenas a full confession of his crimes, meaning a signed statement saying he regretted having written novels and short stories critical of communism.

In the end, State Security achieved its pathetic goal. After more mistreatment, Arenas signed a statement repudiating his past, a recantation he found deeply demoralizing. He was, however, able to take solace in the fact that he had previously released the statement from Lenin Park making clear that if he ever were to retract his words or prior actions, his change of heart should be ignored because it would be the product of coercion, not conscience. Thus, he had already nullified his own confession, and in this he found a small measure of comfort.

Finally, after forcing his declaration of guilt, the government quickly returned him to El Morro, notified the world press of his presence there, then set a date for his sexual misconduct trial, proceedings, it turns out, that would prove to be unforgettable.

TRIAL AND ERROR

The trial was held in Havana during the summer of 1974. As was common practice during the period, Castro's agents arranged for the proceedings to be televised, with a large studio audience in attendance. The event was orchestrated in such a way as to portray Arenas as an immoral man and dissident writer, albeit one who recently had come to his senses and made amends to the state.

The trial did not unfold as the government had planned, however. When the defendants—the two young men from the beach—sauntered into the courtroom, spectators were taken aback because both were over six feet tall and brawny, their appearance undercutting the accusation that Arenas had taken advantage of two innocent, underage boys. Clearly, these men were no juveniles. Demolishing the state's case entirely, however, was their testimony itself.

When the prosecuting attorney asked the first defendant if the writer had made sexual overtures toward him on the beach several months earlier, the young man replied, "no." The prosecutor, stunned, rephrased the question, this time in more detail, but the defendant simply looked across the courtroom at Arenas and again said no. Crimson faced, the judge himself then jumped to his feet and bellowed, "Did he suck your cock or didn't he?"[21] For the third time, the defendant said no.

Next on the stand was the second young man, whose testimony was even more devastating. Not only did he say that he had never had sex with Arenas or Pepe Malas, he claimed that he was not even at the beach on the day in question. He was not there, he knew nothing—that was his testimony.

Of course, this enraged the judge further. He again broke into the proceedings, this time threatening both young men with charges of perjury, but neither would change his story. According to Arenas's account of the trial, it has never been determined why the defendants lied on the stand, an extremely risky act in light of the vindictiveness of the Castro regime, but lie they did. The spectators, given this startling turn of events, fully expected the charges against Arenas to be dropped and for him to be set free. Cuba was a dictatorship, however, where decisions were based on the whims of autocrats. The judge therefore launched into a tirade about how Arenas was a murderous counterrevolutionary and a seducer of young men, and thus someone who deserved to be locked away, despite the fact that there was no evidence to back up either accusation. Such pesky details notwithstanding, the judge proceeded to drop all charges against Malas, while, in the same breath, ordered Arenas back to prison.

This did not bring the matter to a close, however. Whereas the Cuban government silenced the nation's media on a regular basis, the regime was unable to muzzle the foreign press, which howled at the judge's arbitrary, undemocratic actions against the writer. Of course, the media's outcry fueled the scandal itself. Through its courtroom stunts, the state had unwittingly shown its true colors.

"If anyone should have benefited from the Cuban revolution," writes Francisco Soto, "it would have been a poor country boy who was forced to eat dirt because of a scarcity of food, and who came of age with a revolution intent on righting social wrongs."[22] Instead, Castro's political machine revealed itself to be the oppressor of many of those who were already downtrodden. The Arenas travesty was an example for all the world to see.

Literature and Dissent

As for why Castro and his ilk should have found a writer so threatening, Arenas believed it was because authors, like other creative individuals, offer intensely moving experiences that a totalitarian state cannot duplicate. In the eyes of the state, beautiful, aesthetic experiences are considered dangerous because they reveal the existence of a realm beyond that which the state can impose upon the citizenry.

Another source of threat, Arenas believed, were the ideas he expressed in his writings, as well as his independence in doing so. Certainly it is true that his short stories, poems, and novels alarmed the Cuban government not only because they criticized the efforts of repressive political regimes to restrict human liberty, but also because his writings emphasized the inherent freedom of the body, mind, and spirit. Because Arenas expressed such ideas in print, the government, he believed, perceived that he was deliberately challenging it as a competitor for influencing the mind and soul of the people.

Similar thoughts had been voiced years earlier by Soviet writer Aleksandr Solzhenitsyn, perhaps best known in the West for his masterwork *The Gulag Archipelago,* which recounted the inhumanity he witnessed in Stalin's prison camps. As with Arenas, Solzhenitsyn was both feared and despised by his nation's leaders and was banished from his homeland for over twenty years.

"A great writer is, so to speak, a second government in his country," Solzhenitsyn wrote in *The First Circle.* "And for that reason no regime has ever loved great writers, only minor ones."[23]

Certainly, Arenas was one of the finest and most influential Cuban authors of his time, so it is no wonder he was looked upon as an enemy of the state. He was an authentic artist who heeded his inner voice and expressed himself eloquently during a period when brutal measures were taken against those who dared speak out.

All too often the Castro regime succeeded in muzzling authors. Some of them, intimidated by the government, devolved into puppets of the dictatorship, among other deeds penning works worshipful of Fidel Castro. Worse still, these same men and women blew the whistle on their colleagues—dissident writers—who were in hiding, in fear for their lives. In other cases, authors of sounder principle, appalled by the Communist state, stopped writing altogether rather than permit their literary creations to be regulated by the regime. Then there was a handful of writers, among them Reinaldo Arenas, who insisted on writing even at the risk of imprisonment, torture, or death.

"Art is unthinkable without risk and spiritual self-sacrifice," said Russian novelist Boris Pasternak in a lecture titled "On Modesty and Bravery." Pasternak himself was a nonconformist in his day. Certainly, risk and self-sacrifice were emblematic of Arenas.[24] Even while incarcerated in 1975, he managed to ensure that his third novel, *The Palace of the White Skunks,* was published in France, which was merely one year after his spurious trial and after serving still more time in El Morro prison. At that point, he was consigned to a rehabilitation farm near Havana, where he was forced to put in another year of manual labor. Even in the face of such obstacles, he never stopped creating, and he stepped up his creative efforts in 1976 after he was finally released from custody. Even though penniless and largely alone, he retained the will to oppose the Castro machine, and, just as strongly, he retained the will to write. He carried on, creating his remarkable canon of works in a Cuba that had changed immeasurably since his arrest.

The Consequences of Confinement

Upon his release, Arenas discovered that his incarceration had struck fear in the hearts of Cuban writers, along with anxiety and dread in the gay and lesbian citizenry. He realized, too, that he had become something of a pariah. The Cuban Writers and Artists Union, for instance, the organization to which he had contributed so much over the years, now recoiled from him, as did many former friends and colleagues who believed it politically unwise to associate with him. Understandably, their unfaithfulness both hurt and enraged him, pain he ultimately transformed into art.

Years later he wrote a futuristic novel, *El asalto* (The Assault), about an Orwellian society whose members are so dehumanized they do not have names. They also do not form personal relationships.

"Most people," says the novel's anonymous protagonist,

> fearing that some acquaintance of theirs might one day be sentenced to Total Annihilation and therefore take with him anyone that knows him, now avoid any sort of relationship or acquaintance, any sort of friendship. . . . Almost no one knows the person beside them at work—nor is anyone interested. . . . Nobody knows anybody. They are *disacquainted.*[25]

As with the citizens of that fictitious realm, Arenas found himself disacquainted by those who had long known him and he was none too happy about it. One acquaintance who did appear to remain loyal to him, however, was writer Norberto Fuentes, who invited Arenas to live with him upon his release from prison. It soon became evident, however, that Fuentes was himself a pawn of Fidel Castro. State Security, it seems, had advised him to open his home to Arenas, then use the arrangement to siphon information from him. Sadly, Fuentes had agreed. Disgusted by such shameless double-dealing, Arenas promptly moved out and took a room at the Montserrat Hotel, a former brothel, where he carried on writing while performing odd jobs to survive.

In the ensuing years, he found himself disheartened much of the time as well as concerned about his safety, a fear that was not unfounded. Writers such as Arenas who had expressed unpopular views were now disappearing or turning up dead, among them his friend and mentor Virgilio Piñera. Although State Security, which took possession of Piñera's corpse, claimed he died of a heart attack, the organization never released his body. For this reason, an independent autopsy could not be performed nor could acquaintances view his remains.

Unnerved by such shady affairs, Arenas secretly dispatched a letter to Jorge and Margarita Comachos in Paris pleading for their help in escaping. The messenger he chose, however, turned out to be yet another Castro informer—they were everywhere, it seems—who gave the letter to a newspaper. Published under the headline, "Reinaldo Arenas Threatens Suicide If Not Helped Out of Cuba," the document did nothing to improve the writer's relationship with the regime, but it did alert Castro to Arenas's intention to flee the island.[26]

By the beginning of 1980, Arenas was feeling more distraught than ever. He believed his youth was behind him and that his future was bleak. He was saddened because he had never tasted freedom and suspected that he would never do so. Then the Peruvian Embassy incident occurred, the one depicted at the beginning of this chapter, and at once his fortune changed.

Although Arenas was not among those who charged into the embassy, a friend told him he could claim otherwise and receive an exit permit from the Cuban government provided he could prove he was an "antisocial" citizen. Of course, this was simple enough. Arenas took his prison certificate along with documents accusing him of homosexual conduct to a policy jury in Havana, which reviewed them, then scrawled his name on the list of approved emigrants. Fortunately for Arenas, they were unaware of his fame as a writer, which is not surprising considering that only one of his books had ever been published in Cuba, and then had swiftly been banned. Following this chain of events, government agents arrived at his apartment a few days later and ordered him to leave on the Mariel Boatlift.

STORM IN THE STATES

After a turbulent journey at sea that lasted two weeks, the boat carrying Arenas docked in Key West, where he learned the Castro regime was scouring Cuba for him. It had awakened to its mistake and was now making every effort to track down and prevent him from leaving the country, but it was too late. He was now in the United States, and his whereabouts quickly made world news. In the months that followed, his actions continued to make headlines, quite often in a scandalous manner. Although he had finally found freedom in a democratic nation, he remained the subject of debate due to his unabashed homosexuality and his spirited opposition to the Castro administration.

After settling in Miami, for instance, Arenas at once began denouncing the dictator, which aggravated scores of left-wing intellectuals who approved of Castro's deeds in Cuba. At the same time, he upset many right-wing figures because he turned his back on the mantle of celebrity the Miami social elite sought to bestow upon him. He later explained that he was put off by the superficiality of high society.

He moved to Manhattan on New Year's Eve, 1981, and instantly fell under its charm largely because of the anonymity it offered, along with its inspiring assortment of gay men. Never one to sit idly by when it came to erotic opportunities, Arenas quickly threw himself into sex with a gusto he had not enjoyed since his halcyon days on Cuba's beaches. Routinely, he picked up men on 42nd Street, cruised Central Park, and pursued African Americans in Harlem—he always had a penchant for fine looking black men. He even took an apartment in one of the city's more explicit areas, Hell's Kitchen, where he quickly established a reputation as a player.

"His sexual appetite was voracious," recalled an acquaintance, novelist Jaime Manrique. "Coming home late at night I would see him prowling Times Square or walking out of the sleaziest sex joints."[27]

Although Arenas was spending his nights in the embrace of men, he still spent his days denouncing Fidel Castro and the Cuban Revolution. By all accounts, his harrowing experiences on the island had altered his psyche indelibly, leaving him with a conviction to help those still suffering under the dictatorship. As in Miami, he soon found himself embroiled in conflict over the Cuban situation.

During a lecture he attended at New York University, for instance, a speech delivered by an admirer of the dictator moved Arenas to jump to his feet and call the speaker "a lying son of a bitch."[28] Leftists in the ballroom grabbed Arenas, flung him into the air, and pinned him against a wall, but he refused to apologize. Predictably, the next day's headlines trumpeted the fiasco, and the Latin American community thereafter cringed at the mere mention of the debacle.

On another occasion, Arenas was himself the guest speaker at Harvard University where he attended a lavish banquet in his honor. In the course of the event, he met a professor from Germany who made the grave mistake of praising the Castro regime, even though he had never stepped foot in Cuba and knew little about life on the island. Arenas, alluding to the gourmet food the man had selected for himself, told him that in Cuba most people would never experience such a meal—except for Castro and his friends. He then picked up the professor's plate and threw it against the wall.

As such confrontations demonstrate, Arenas did not hesitate to speak bluntly about his ordeal in the totalitarian state and had little patience with non-Cubans who feigned familiarity with the Castro regime, or, worse still, advocated it. After the traumas he endured under the Communist system, he did not suffer fools gladly. So with torture in his past and a fiery temper in the present, he came to be regarded as a walking powder keg, albeit a brilliant one.

In addition, being unapologetically gay caused him to be at odds with certain blocs, most notably conservative Cuban Americans and the Hispanic literati, both of whom preferred he not discuss or write about homosexuality, including his own. They believed it reflected negatively on Latin America and detracted from his status as an author. Yet their views only angered Arenas, who argued that those who passed such judgments were like Castro himself, in that they attempted to silence those different from themselves.

The writer, within a few short years, found himself alienated and depressed once again, although not as severely as he had been in Cuba.

He was much more content living in a democracy, despite its short-comings, because as he explained, he could at least voice his displeasure in such a society without being imprisoned or killed for it. He was further convinced that he was more able to achieve his potential in the United States.

Certainly, as an American citizen, Arenas was finally able to visit France, the nation that had made his early works available to the world, as well as Sweden, Denmark, Spain, Portugal, and Venezuela. He also contributed to four documentary films about political oppression in Cuba and cofounded the Spanish language magazine *Mariel,* an entire issue of which he devoted to the problem of gay and lesbian persecution. In addition, he received three distinguished fellowships, a Guggenheim among them, and spoke at over forty colleges and universities. As if this were not enough, he wrote and published still more books, all within a decade of his arrival at Key West.

Regrettably, however, Arenas also contracted HIV shortly after his arrival, at a time when the infection was little understood and its medical management was limited. As could be expected, the condition sapped his energy and diminished his morale, which caused him to conclude that he had at last encountered a challenge he would be unable to surmount. He kept moving forward nonetheless. Among other achievements, he used his remaining years to complete several written works, including the memoir he had begun while hiding in Lenin Park two decades earlier.

Finally, on an cold winter's day in 1990, the writer, aware that his demise was imminent yet appeased that his literary work was now complete, brought his life to a close with a bottle of Chivas Regal and a handful of pills. Still, Arenas did not go gently into the night. In a parting shot directed at the Cuban regime—his last act of political protest—he sent a letter to several friends, with copies to the police, the Cuban émigré community, and *The New York Times.* It read, in part,

> The sufferings of exile, the pain of being banished from my country, the loneliness, and the diseases contracted in exile would probably never have happened if I had been able to enjoy freedom in my country. . . . There is only one person I hold accountable: Fidel Castro."[29]

"Cuba will be free," he said. "I already am."[30]

Chapter 7

A Charge of Libel:
Kaiser Wilhelm II
and the Eulenburg Affair

At the mouth of the Bay of Naples sits the island of Capri, a geographic jewel hailed throughout history for its splendor. In Greek mythology, it was said to be the home of the Sirens, those mystical maidens whose music lured love-drunk sailors to their deaths along the island's jagged shores. In 1902, however, Capri's allure led another man to his ruin, and this time he was no mythical invention.

In the late nineteenth and early twentieth centuries, the island's majestic grottos and sapphire-blue lagoons attracted a stream of wealthy, well-heeled tourists from Europe, among them a prominent German business tycoon named Friedrich "Fritz" Alfred Krupp. Married and the heir to a family fortune amassed in the steel industry, Krupp often traveled to Capri to savor its rugged beauty and partake of its fine wines. He also immersed himself in another of its charms: its men, young Adonises who were quite handsome and, in some cases, sexually available to foreign visitors willing to reward them for their affections. Krupp became one such visitor, but before long, he also became a problem for Capri. It seems his sexual encounters became so excessive and ultimately so scandalous that the authorities felt compelled to bar him from the island.

Krupp's banishment did not bring to an end his erotic shopping trips. Krupp continued cruising the Mediterranean in search of sunny young lovers, the most desirable of whom he supplied with letters of introduction to elegant hotels across Europe which would then employ them as staff members. One of these was a swank Berlin establishment known as the Bristol. Bowing to Krupp's wealth, the Bristol hired his foreign paramours to perform standard hotel services with the understanding that whenever Krupp came to stay, they would be excused from their duties so they could join in his private sex parties; an arrangement that, despite its boldness, did not raise eyebrows among the chic Berliners who peopled Krupp's world.

The fact is, certain segments of German society were remarkably accepting of same-sex relations in that era, and male homosexuality in particular was practiced rather widely by military officers and members of the ruling class. It was well known in certain circles, for instance, that the King of Bavaria fancied his coachman and the King of Wurtemberg had an eye for his mechanic. Although homosexuality was so prevalent among the upper class that it came to be known abroad as the "German vice," the topic was seldom mentioned in public. As with other aspects of personal life, same-sex liaisons were considered private matters. There was, however, a militant political faction accruing power at that time called the Social Democratic Party that hoped to make homosexuality a very public issue. A fervent socialist group, it sought to expose the homosexuality of Germany's moneyed elite so the populace could behold the "corruption" of that segment of society. To this end, the Party initiated the practice of outing in Germany and selected Fritz Krupp as its first target.

To expose him, the left-wing newspaper, *Vorwarts* (Forward), published an article that described the millionaire's indiscretions on Capri and the reasons behind his expulsion from the island, and recounted some of his more outlandish sexual antics at home in Germany. In response, Krupp frantically denied the allegations and then went to considerable lengths to hide the evidence, a predictable course of events given his towering stature in German society. Panicked and desperate, he even went so far as to commit his wife to a mental institution for fear she might speak out about his gay past. Even with his spouse removed from the scene, the racy stories continued to circulate. Realizing he would be unable to stop the spread of the risqué, but altogether true, accounts of his unorthodox sex life and realizing he was facing a possible court trial, the magnate killed himself.

In a rather ghoulish reaction, the Social Democratic Party cheered his suicide as a victory for the people. In addition, the Party became emboldened by it and was further convinced that outings would help ensure a successful outcome for their movement. So it was, writes Neil Miller, that "rapidly the use of accusations of homosexuality to destroy political opponents became a characteristic of Imperial German politics."[1] This unsavory drama would not be played out in the mainstream press, however, until a few years later.

Indeed, one of the more extraordinary aspects of the Krupp scandal is that the German press, despite the actions of a few leftist publications such as *Vorwarts,* chose not to examine the charges against the industrialist. Instead, throughout the affair the media either refused to report the story at all or, ignoring the mountainous evidence against Krupp, staunchly defended him against the allegations of sexual misconduct. The mainstream press, it seems, had long been loath to print damaging personal information about illustrious national figures, and opted instead to protect the reputations of those who were rich and powerful. The press certainly did not hesitate to condemn *Vorwarts'* coverage of the episode, however, decrying the newspaper's cutting exposé as a work of unparalleled savagery. Unbowed, the Social Democratic Party, in the years following the Krupp incident, continued gathering ruinous homosexual material to use against its political enemies while the mainstream press persistently refused to repeat the accusations. All of this was to change, however, with the Eulenburg Affair, a national scandal that turned sex in high places into front-page headlines, and in so doing altered the lives of countless German citizens, among them Kaiser Wilhelm II.

THE KAISER'S GAY ENTOURAGE

The ultimate target of the Eulenburg Affair, Kaiser Wilhelm II, was born in 1859 in Berlin, the son of Emperor Frederick III and his wife Victoria, daughter of Queen Victoria of England. In 1881, after serving in the military, young Wilhelm married a German princess, then seven years later ascended to the position of kaiser, or emperor, after his father's death.

Unfortunately, soon after taking the reins he infuriated a powerful political figure who thereafter became a formidable adversary, Otto von Bismarck, the esteemed "Iron Chancellor," whose brilliance helped build the German empire into a major political and economic force. Bismarck, stunned and indignant, resigned because of their dispute and subsequently nursed an enduring hatred for the kaiser. Furthermore, this enmity prompted him to reveal to the leader's critics the unconventional sexual activities known to be taking place behind the palace doors. One of these critics was Maximilian Harden, a middle-class Jewish publisher with an intense interest in national affairs.

As with Bismarck, Harden disapproved of the kaiser, whose poor judgment, he was convinced, would steer Germany to its ruin. Accordingly, Harden set out to undermine Wilhelm's authority by gathering, throughout the 1890s and early 1900s, unflattering political and personal information about him and his associates. Harden obtained the information from the likes of Otto von Bismarck and from palace servants, disgruntled officials, and one particularly fertile source of gossip, Baron Friedrich von Holstein, whom the kaiser had previously fired from his position as First Councilor.

Harden did not sit on the information he had acquired, but quickly put it to use. Among other projects, he wrote and published a small, weekly newspaper, *Die Zukunft* (The Future), which dissected—and berated—the leader's domestic and foreign policies. Harden was careful to ensure that the articles focused on political issues, not intimate matters. Although he was opinionated and defiant, the publisher was smart enough to realize that attacking the kaiser on a personal level would be foolhardy; one simply did not criticize the leader's character or lay open his private life. In due time, the publisher became so obsessed with Wilhelm's political incompetence that he was determined to bring him down for the sake of the empire. He concocted a scheme whereby he could injure the kaiser's credibility without directly baring his private life. Harden's plan was to use *Die Zukunft* to mangle the reputations of the kaiser's closest friends and political cronies, and in this way tarnish Wilhelm by association. Thus began a series of smear campaigns in which the number-one target on Harden's hit list was a good-natured man born into nobility and the kaiser's oldest and most adored companion, sixty-year-old Prince Philipp zu Eulenburg-Hertefeld.

Kaiser Wilhelm II and Philipp Eulenburg first met in 1886, attracted to one another, they said, by their mutual love of music and the visual arts. Eulenburg, at the time, was a married man, stately and handsome, a talented gentleman who composed music and wrote plays and children's books. Over the next two decades, he and the kaiser nurtured a deep friendship, shared much time together, and gave their relationship priority over other personal attachments, including their own marriages. Furthermore, although the kaiser eventually appointed Eulenburg to two important diplomatic posts, most notably to an ambassadorship in Vienna, their bond remained based on affection, not politics.

Perhaps inevitably, given their obvious fondness for one another, their relationship soon came to be viewed by others as a romantic one. Even Otto von Bismarck, before his departure from office, wrote in a letter to his son that the nature of the two men's attachment could "not be confided to paper."[2] If Eulenburg and the kaiser were indeed in love, this, in itself, does not mean they had sex. "Romantic friendships" were fairly common in those days, relationships that, although erotically nuanced, were never actually consummated. It is known, however, that Eulenburg later developed a full sexual relationship with another man, an official of the kaiser, and that it was this attachment Maximilian Harden set out to expose. By revealing it, the publisher believed he could degrade the public image of Kaiser Wilhelm II, since the scandal would incriminate Philipp Eulenburg, his most treasured friend and ally, and Count Kuno von Moltke, the military commandant of Berlin under the kaiser's rule.

The Eulenburg Exposé

To ignite the scandal, Harden published a pair of articles in 1906 and 1907 that declared two prominent men situated close to Wilhelm were having an affair. Although the articles did not mention their names, Harden made sure to drop enough hints that within a short time the public had figured out their identities.

In these cynical pieces, Harden ridiculed Moltke's *susslichkeit* or "sweetness," even going so far as to nickname him "Sweetie" in the articles, an allusion not only to the commandant's liking for chocolate but also a German slang term for an effeminate gay man. Since the publisher had already revealed Moltke's real nickname, "Tutu," in an earlier article, he invented this new one to further mock the man's homosexuality. As for Philipp Eulenburg, Harden had previously branded him the "leader of a sinister and effeminate cammarilla," so now he dubbed the music-loving aristocrat "the Harpist" and caricatured Eulenburg's longtime attachment to the commandant.[3] He even devised a scenario in which Sweetie and the Harpist coyly discuss a mutual gay friend they call "Darling," who was none other than Kaiser Wilhelm II himself.

Of course, by printing such muck, Harden had crossed a line in publishing. By deliberately revealing the homosexuality of influential political figures, says historian Alexandra Richie, he "broke one of the most sacred taboos in imperial Germany."[4] And the consequences were staggering.

The citizenry, most notably the middle class who was heretofore blind to the fact that those in the upper echelon were enjoying same-sex relations with some frequency, was stunned, titillated, but mostly outraged that the kaiser's court contained powerful men who were in love with one another. More important, the public now questioned the kaiser's own sexual orientation, as well as his judgment in selecting friends and officials such as Eulenburg and Moltke, men Harden portrayed as lovesick, distracted, and dysfunctional. Of course, this was precisely the public reaction Harden had hoped to provoke.

As for the kaiser's response to the exposé, because he refused, on principle, to read anything printed in *Die Zukunft,* his son, the crown prince and a closeted gay man himself, read the defamatory essays to him. Reportedly shocked by the use of the word *homosexual* in the articles, Wilhelm was said to be mortified upon learning that Eulenburg and Moltke might be gay. Feigning moral revulsion, he at once distanced himself from his old friend (and possibly former lover) Philipp Eulenburg, as well as from Kuno von Moltke. In addition, determined to safeguard his image and preserve his political power, he demanded that Eulenburg either clear himself of the accusations or surrender his estate and leave Germany. The kaiser commanded Moltke to resign his commission. In this way, Wilhelm not only shielded himself from the smear, but actually scored points with the public, which came to regard him as a bold leader because of the firmness with which he dealt with the two men. For the moment, at least, the citizenry's concerns about the kaiser had been put to rest.

Philipp Eulenburg's reaction to the exposé and to the kaiser's callous, self-serving betrayal of him was one of disappointment and fear. Initially, he fled to Switzerland, where, upon arriving, he hired a courier to return to Germany and inform Harden that he had left the country, an impulsive, desperate move designed to put an end to the intrusions into his personal life. He soon reconsidered his decision and returned to Germany, secured a lawyer, and set out to absolve himself. To this end, it appears the aristocrat forged an agreement with the sympathetic district attorney in his hometown. It worked this way: Eulenburg would acknowledge being gay and violating Paragraph 175 of the German penal code, the law criminalizing "unnatural vice" between men. The district attorney would accept Eulenburg's confession, review the matter, then dismiss all of the charges against him, including that of homosexual conduct. In this way, Eulenburg's name would be legally cleared. Indeed, these events did come to pass, but Eulenburg's reputation, in tatters by that time, was never fully restored.

By comparison, Kuno von Moltke chose to fight the charges against him, a decision that heightened and prolonged the scandal. First and foremost, Moltke claimed, falsely, that he was not gay, and that he and his friend Philipp Eulenburg had never been lovers, another untruth. Second, he sued Maximilian Harden in civil court on a libel charge, arguing that the publisher purposefully set out to destroy his reputation, a grievance that culminated in the most celebrated trial of its kind in the history of Berlin and prompted further lawsuits.

THE TRIALS

The *Moltke vs. Harden* case was the first of six legal proceedings which stemmed directly or indirectly from the Eulenburg Affair, and, as such, was the event that shattered the public silence about homosexuality. Unfortunately, one unforeseen consequence of this new candor was that it permitted even more accusations to pour forth in the ensuing months.

"German newspapers were suddenly full of the story," writes historian James Steakley, "and it dominated their headlines for months; an anti-homosexual witch-hunt of unparalleled proportions was unleashed. Nearly every high government official and military officer was suspected or accused of homosexuality."[5] To be sure, the scandal became a political and legal nightmare.

The Moltke vs. Harden *Trials*

In *Moltke vs. Harden,* the proceedings commenced on October 23, 1907, with Harden, the defendant, setting the tone of the event by

declaring that the kaiser's palace was suffering from a "heady romantic atmosphere"; an amorous milieu, he insisted, that was clouding
the political judgment and actions of those in power, specifically Kaiser Wilhelm II.[6] Using Eulenburg and Moltke to exemplify this ro-
manticism (and to defend himself against Moltke's charge of libel),
Harden read aloud an eyewitness account of the two men's clandestine meetings in a forest, encounters that were unmistakably sexual.
His lawyers then called over sixty witnesses to substantiate the publisher's claim of erotic excesses in the palace and of the sexual bond
between Eulenburg and Moltke.

One of these witnesses was a fisherman who testified that, when he
was seventeen years old, he accepted money for using his boat to take
noblemen onto a lake where the men would have sex together. Although his testimony did not apply directly to Moltke or Eulenburg, it
did help stain their images as German bluebloods since Eulenburg
was a prince and Moltke was a count.

Another witness, a young soldier by the name of Bollhardt, provided testimony that was more damaging. Under oath, he swore that
officers in his regiment in Potsdam routinely had sex with enlistees.
He added that gay sex parties were not uncommon, gatherings held at
private villas teeming with champagne and influential men. Bollhardt
then admitted to having attended some of these parties, where he had
encountered, among others, Kuno von Moltke.

Of course, such salacious material electrified the proceedings,
huge crowds assembled in the courtroom each morning to hear the
racy tales, and press coverage expanded dramatically over the course
of the trial. By that point in the scandal, the whole matter of male homosexuality had been opened to public discourse, such that the press,
formerly the protector of the ruling class, now scrambled for the intimate details of the trial.

Certainly, the media relished the testimony of the star witness for
the defense, Lili von Elbe, the ex-wife of Kuno von Moltke. A divorcée
with a young son when she married the commandant, their union
lasted only two years. At the time of the trial, the couple had been divorced nine years and Lili had remarried for the third time.

When she and Moltke decided to wed, she recalled, Philipp Eulenburg vigorously opposed their plan. Over his objections, they married, and during the first two nights of their honeymoon, made love. It
would be the last time they did so, however. Lili said Moltke there-

after refused to have sex with her, going so far as to place a pan of water between them in bed so she could not make sexual advances during the night. She further claimed that her husband, throughout their marriage, spent nearly all of his time with Eulenburg, including family holidays such as Christmas. She also recalled an incident in which Moltke found his friend's handkerchief, held it to his lips, and muttered "Phili, my Phili," a man he described as "my soulmate, my old boy, my one and only cuddly bear."[7] Lili added that her ten-year-old son had taken to mimicking Moltke behind his back.

Another witness embraced by the press was Magnus Hirschfeld, the gay physician, renowned sex researcher, and chairman of the Scientific Humanitarian Committee, a group created to fight for the repeal of the German antihomosexuality law. Hirschfeld declared that, in his expert judgment, Moltke was, in fact, gay, as Harden had written in his exposé, an opinion the researcher formed on the basis of Lili von Elbe's testimony about her ex-husband. Hirschfeld added that his personal observations of Moltke's conduct during the trial supported his belief that the commandant was homosexual; for instance, he noticed Moltke was wearing cosmetics in the courtroom. Such was the occasionally farcical flavor of the defense.

Moltke's lawyers simply could not compete. Their presentation lacked the energy, the theatrics, and the sheer number of witnesses provided by Harden's legal team. They even failed to call Philipp Eulenburg, a key figure in the case. Worsening the matter, Magnus Hirschfeld was not alone in inferring a person's sexual orientation on the basis of physical appearances. Moltke's demeanor during the trial led many spectators to likewise conclude he was gay.

Finally, after six days of testimony, a verdict was handed down. The magistrate, convinced that Moltke was indisputably homosexual, acquitted Harden of the libel charge. Since the publisher's politically motivated sexual exposé was apparently built on fact, he could not be prosecuted. To most everyone's surprise, this was not the end of the case. Although Germany's middle class was satisfied with the outcome, many observers could not bear the histrionics of some of the defense's key witnesses, most notably the performance of Lili von Elbe. They doubted the soundness of her testimony. Moreover, several powerful citizens were deeply shaken by the fact that a bourgeois Jewish publisher could attack, in print, members of the ruling class and get away with it. Their fear was that the mainstream press might increasingly target the private lives of other prominent Germans such as themselves; the media was being viewed, more and more, as aggressive and unconstrained. Even the judiciary believed it had erred, troubled that the verdict might somehow corrode the citizenry's faith in the empire. A technical flaw was quickly discovered in a review of the trial proceedings, so the verdict was thrown out and a retrial ordered.

On December 18, 1907, a new trial commenced and the charge against Harden was upgraded from civil libel to criminal libel, a more serious indictment. During these proceedings, Lili von Elbe's testimony was discounted because medical professionals had since diagnosed her as hysterical, meaning that her perception of events was unreliable. Magnus Hirschfeld, as a result, withdrew his testimony since it had been based primarily on Lili's account of her former marriage. For this reason, the esteemed sex researcher became something of a public joke, an expert witness who had relied on the recollections of a classic hysteric to arrive at a professional opinion. Finally, both Philipp Eulenburg and Kuno von Moltke testified at the trial and insisted they were not gay but rather extolled the virtues of that noble German tradition, male friendship, which they painstakingly sought to distinguish from homosexuality.

Two weeks later, when all of the new testimony had been heard, the magistrate delivered his verdict: Moltke's homosexuality had not, in fact, been established by the court, therefore Maximilian Harden was judged guilty of criminal libel. As punishment, Harden was sentenced to four months in prison. For the moment, it seemed, the privileged class had been spared. Among its members, however, the worry persisted that they might yet become the targets of future exposés. Their fears were soon validated as other gay sex scandals erupted just as the Moltke trial was winding down, an uproar that might never have occurred had the Eulenburg Affair not created such a fanatical, litigious atmosphere.

The fact is, prior to and during the *Moltke vs. Harden* trial, several prominent men were publicly accused of homosexuality, some of whom were also the victims of extortion. Major Johannes von Lynar, for instance, a nobleman and military officer, was ordered to resign his commission because he was rumored to be sexually intimate with his male aide-de-camp. Lieutenant General Hohenau, also a nobleman and a relative of Kaiser Wilhelm II, was likewise commanded to relinquish his commission due to his purported same-sex activities. Between 1906 and 1907, six soldiers committed suicide because they were being blackmailed for having sex with men.[8]

The allegations did not stop with the military. Those in the arts were targeted as well, a profession long known to have a substantial gay membership and one that had been respectfully left alone in the past. Among the casualties was Georg von Julsen, the manager of Berlin's Royal Theatre, who was accused of being romantically involved with the crown prince's male assistant. Then there were those men who decided to come forward on their own. Determined not to live with the constant dread of exposure, a handful of powerful gay figures, most notably the Prince of Prussia, became more open about their same-sex activities.

Without a doubt, charges of homosexuality and countercharges of libel were becoming rampant as a result of the Eulenburg incident, accusations that increasingly ended up in court. This was certainly the case for the allegations cast by an extremist named Adolf Brand. A spin-off of the Eulenburg Affair, the Brand scandal sought to expose the same-sex activities of a key official, while at the same time further blackening the reputation of Philipp Eulenburg. The result was another highly publicized, and important, libel trial.

The Bulow vs. Brand *Trial*

Adolf Brand was a lifelong married man and former teacher who left the profession to become an editor, publisher, and gay activist. In 1896, he founded the world's first gay male periodical, *Der Eigene* (One's Own), for which he was twice arrested on obscenity charges. He also strove to mobilize Germany's homosexual citizenry for political action, believing that only a mass movement could win lasting equality. In *Der Eigene,* he wrote,

> We must demonstrate to our enemies that we are men and that, in numbers and intelligence, we stand for such a considerable power in the state that, once having become capable of action, we can no longer be bypassed at all in the deciding of important cultural questions![9]

Like Magnus Hirschfeld before him, Brand formed an organization to fight for the repeal of Germany's antihomosexuality law. Unlike Hirschfeld's intelligent reserve, Brand was an angry, impulsive, and reckless man who did not hesitate to expose gay people, arguing that such revelations could help overturn the empire's antigay injunction. Calling his dubious campaign the "path over corpses," he insisted that outing was necessary if the gay population's quality of life was ever to equal that of the heterosexual citizenry.[10] There must be martyrs, he declared. One of those he tried to sacrifice was the new chancellor of Germany himself, Prince Bernhard von Bulow.

In a leaflet Brand wrote and circulated, Bulow was accused of having an affair with Privy Councilor Scheefer, his male secretary. To back up the charge, he claimed that Bulow had been seen kissing his secretary at one of Philipp Eulenburg's exclusive sex parties. Even more damning, he accused the chancellor of having surrendered to blackmail in order to conceal the relationship, a grave charge given the official's position. Last, he argued that it was Bulow's duty as a gay man to come forward and fight for the repeal of Germany's antigay law. The chancellor, however, felt differently. Rather than fight for the reversal of the empire's law against homosexuality, he chose to do battle with Adolf Brand himself, and so pressed criminal libel charges against him.

The trial took place on November 6, 1907. It was a major legal event and a public spectacle—a capacity crowd jammed the courtroom and spilled into the hallways—and the trial ended the same day it began. This is because the verdict was largely a foregone conclusion. It seems the citizenry, initially angry at the targets of such exposés, was now becoming weary and resentful of those setting up the exposés themselves. Apparently the German people were beginning to yearn for the old days when homosexuality was not discussed in public, when it was not widely known that officials were having sex with one another. It was this prevailing mood that doomed Adolf Brand in the courtroom.

Serving as his own defense, the activist took the stand and swore that his statements about Chancellor Bulow had been true, that the man was gay and had been blackmailed because of it. Partial support for his accusation of extortion was provided by Berlin's chief of the vice division, but this official's testimony proved to be rather unpopular—it was not what the court wanted to hear—and so was disregarded. Brand further argued that his writings had not been libelous, that he had done nothing illegal in stating that a gay man was, indeed, a gay man.

Chancellor Bulow, in his testimony, coolly denied all of Brand's accusations, said he was not gay, had not been the victim of extortion, and had not kissed his male secretary at a sex party hosted by Philipp Eulenburg. Insisting he had never attended such a gathering, Bulow said his personal reputation was impeccable. He added, however, that the same could not be said of Eulenburg; a cheap shot at a fellow gay man and a self-serving maneuver designed to place distance between the chancellor and Eulenburg, a controversial figure at the time.

Finally, Eulenburg took the stand. Ignoring Bulow's calculated remark, he testified, as before, that he was not gay. He added that he had never hosted a gay sex party nor seen Bulow kiss his male secretary.

After a brief recess, the judge returned with the verdict. He found Adolf Brand guilty of criminal libel and sentenced him to eighteen months in jail, a swift judgment and a harsh sentence.

Of course, it is important to bear in mind that Philipp Eulenburg, Kuno von Moltke, and Bernhard von Bulow, all married men, were indeed actively homosexual despite their repeated public denials. It is also important to note that the German courts were complicit in these men's efforts to conceal their gay lives. More often than not, the verdicts were not intended to reveal the truth or deliver justice, but to protect the facade of the ruling class' heterosexuality. It is for this reason that Eulenburg, Moltke, and von Bulow initially won their cases.

The trials revealed something else, something beyond the complicity of the judicial system. They revealed the growing disdain of the public and the ruling class in regard to the media's increasing tendency to infringe upon the privacy of the citizenry for purely political purposes. This widespread aversion did not stop the media's assaults, however, nor did it diminish the militancy of publisher Maximilian Harden, who, after his release from prison, once again resumed his attacks on the kaiser's friends and associates. As before, he began by assailing Philipp Eulenburg.

The Harden vs. Stadele *Trial*

With his latest set of allegations, Harden was shamelessly underhanded. Enraged, vindictive, and convinced that Eulenburg had engaged in gay sex and lied about it during the two previous trials, he intended to see to it that the aristocrat was prosecuted for perjury. By this time, however, the judiciary was no longer keen on pursuing cases related to the Eulenburg Affair; the whole matter had become too unpopular. Harden therefore devised a scheme that would force the court to take action.

"In an elaborate legal ruse," says Steakley, "Harden colluded with an ally, the Bavarian editor Anton Stadele, who published a fraudulent article alleging that Harden had received a million marks in hush money from Eulenburg to desist in his attacks."[11] This bogus accusation of bribery was a clever ploy designed to provide Harden an opportunity to sue his accomplice, Stadele, for libel and generate a trial that would direct public attention back to Philipp Eulenburg's sex life. In this way, the publisher would again be able to present damaging material about the kaiser's friend and confidant.

Held on April 21, 1908, the trial, to Eulenburg's disadvantage, was situated in Munich rather than Berlin. Also to his detriment, Harden's attorneys provided two male witnesses who would testify they had slept with Eulenburg, despite the fact that the case was supposedly about the alleged bribery of Harden, not the homosexuality of the prince. Again, the ulterior purpose of the proceedings was to place Eulenburg's private life on display.

One of these witnesses, a man named Jakob Ernst, was a farmer, a fisherman, and a respected member of his Bavarian community. Initially unwilling to testify, Ernst, with much encouragement from the magistrate, swore under oath that twenty-five years earlier when he was a young soldier, he and Eulenburg had engaged in sex together, an encounter that had led to a long-term affair. Furthermore, although the farmer later married, he continued the romance, portraying the trysts themselves as simple fun. "I don't know of no real name for it," he said. "When we went rowing we just did it in the boat."[12] Ernst added that his wife and friends were aware of his intimate friendship with the prince and were impressed by it. Eulenburg took Ernst on holiday to such cities as Rome and Zurich and, on one occasion, to the pyramids of Egypt. The guileless farmer said their relationship had come to an end only recently.

The second witness was a milkman from Munich who testified that when he was a young man in the military, he, too, had been sexually intimate with Eulenburg. He further claimed that the prince had given him money on occasion and had once introduced him to Kuno von Moltke.

Because of such testimony, Eulenburg's reputation was smeared anew. The official reason for the trial—the purported bribery dispute—became but an afterthought. Regardless, the proceedings wrapped up quickly, and the magistrate convicted Anton Stadele of libel. He was ordered to pay Harden a relatively modest sum in damages, money that Harden no doubt reimbursed the Bavarian editor as had surely been their prior arrangement. Naturally, Harden was pleased with the results of the trial. Not only did they provide the public with bracing new evidence of the supposedly degenerate character of one of the kaiser's closest friends, but the court, having reestablished Eulenburg's homosexuality, overturned the verdict of the earlier *Moltke vs. Harden* retrial and ordered a second one. As for Eulenburg, he was indicted on a perjury charge, which led to one of the last trials of the scandal.

The Final Trials

On June 29, 1908, the proceedings against Eulenburg on the charge of perjury commenced. Along with letters and books seized from his private estate, thirty-six witnesses were lined up to attest to his same-sex activities, ranging from a handful of policemen to a household servant who claimed to have watched through a keyhole while Eulenburg had sex with men. Even his former lover, the farmer and reluctant witness Jakob Ernst, was compelled to testify again. At one point, beside himself with anxiety, Ernst blurted out to Eulenburg from across the courtroom, "By God Almighty, Your Excellency, you can't deny that we two did it." He added, darkly, "We two haven't got a chance in the world."[13]

Then something unexpected happened. Soon after the trial began, Eulenburg claimed to be ill to the point of having to be carried in and out of the courtroom on a stretcher. For this reason, he was granted a suspension of the proceedings. As for whether he was truly ailing, his supporters claimed he was suffering from a debilitating combination of rheumatoid arthritis and heart disease, while his critics insisted he was malingering. In reality, there may be elements of truth to both views. Whatever the actual nature of his illness, the trial resumed a month later in Eulenburg's hospital room, where the list of witnesses was reduced to only two men, both of whom were boatmen from the Munich area.

One of these gentlemen had been a servant at the Eulenburg estate where, he said, two decades earlier he and the aristocrat had enjoyed sex together in a boat. The other man, a scoundrel with thirty-two prior convictions, claimed that he, too, had once engaged in sex with Eulenburg. This same man also attempted to blackmail the prince during the course of the trial, thus undermining the witness' already flimsy credibility.

Perhaps predictably, Eulenburg fell ill again during this gathering in his hospital room, so the proceedings were postponed a second time. It continued this way for many years; the defendant declared illness whenever it came time for his perjury trial and the proceedings were repeatedly suspended, even as Eulenburg returned to his castle and lived in comfort amid the abiding adoration of his domestic staff. In the end, the trial was never concluded. Thirteen years later, in 1921, Philipp Eulenburg died.

The ongoing legal battle between publisher Maximilian Harden and Count Kuno von Moltke was settled in the spring of 1909. At their final trial, Harden was again convicted of libel and ordered to pay damages and court costs to Moltke. Given Harden's history of litigation, he planned to appeal the decision, but was dissuaded from doing so by, among others, Chancellor Bernhard von Bulow, who believed the highly publicized trials were hurting Germany's image in the eyes of the world. Perhaps more important, the trials were hurting von Bulow's own image. Whatever the case, Harden agreed not to pursue the matter if two conditions were met: first, the court would reimburse him the amount he had been fined, and second, it would state for the record that his actions during the three-year scandal had been an expression of his patriotism. The court complied, discreetly refunded his money, and declared publicly that the publisher believed he had acted in the best interests of Germany. With this, the trials stemming from the Eulenburg Affair came to a close. Although the litigation ceased, the scandal itself continued reverberating for years to come.

IMPACT OF THE SCANDAL ON GERMANY

For the players in this drama the winter of 1908 meant emotional strain and physical illness. Suffering from medical ailments were Maximilian Harden, Philipp Eulenburg, Kuno von Moltke, Adolf Brand, Lili von Elbe, and Magnus Hirschfeld. As could be expected, Eulenburg and Moltke, in particular, endured profound stress because their private lives were being thrust into public view, a turn of events they perceived akin to rape. As Eulenburg wrote in a letter to Moltke in the course of the scandal, he felt their opponents had "criticized our nature, stripped our ideal friendship, laid bare the form of our thinking and feeling . . . [and] laughing cold-bloodedly, broke our necks."[14] Devastated, too, was Kaiser Wilhelm II, who, while betraying these same two friends, nonetheless told a third companion that it was excruciating "to see the names of one's friends dragged through all the gutters of Europe without being able or entitled to help."[15] It probably did not help matters that the kaiser was also an old friend (and defender) of Fritz Krupp, the industrialist whose homoerotic escapades with Capri's young men were recounted at the beginning of this chapter. As a result of such personal embarrassments and political pressures, the kaiser suffered what could be described as a nervous breakdown during the Eulenburg trials, and at one point spent two days in bed unable to cope with the maelstrom. To be sure, the whole affair took a remarkable toll on those embroiled in it and occurred at a great cost to the empire itself, in large part because the German media reported the events fully and explicitly, from orgies to extortion.

Indeed, the press, as noted earlier, did not discuss the sexual escapades of public figures until the Eulenburg Affair exploded onto the scene, which it then covered in all-out fashion, its reporting, at times, bordering on the obscene. Many cultural analysts, as a result, bemoaned the trials and their media accounts as having caused a sweeping loss of innocence in German society. Some seized the opportunity to blame specific individuals or groups for undermining the empire. Unfortunately, Jews were among those scapegoated.

Antisemitism

Prior to the Eulenburg Affair there was already brewing in German society a pathological hatred of the Jewish people, and thus it was merely a matter of time before antisemites isolated the scandal's two Jewish participants, Maximilian Harden and Magnus Hirschfeld, and accused them of provoking or abetting the incident. Whereas Harden did indeed ignite the fiasco, Hirschfeld merely appeared in court as a witness and later retracted his testimony. Regardless, both were portrayed as malicious, subversive, and determined to bring down the empire and Hirschfeld, because he was not only Jewish but gay as well, was depicted as particularly dangerous.

This antisemitic rendering of events persisted long after the scandal ended. Following Germany's defeat in World War I, Jews were blamed for the empire's humiliating loss and references were made to the downward spiral triggered by the Eulenburg Affair. Moreover, in the 1920s Kaiser Wilhelm II insisted that the scandal, which he characterized as a plot against the empire, had been set into motion by "international Jewry." Even Adolf Hitler got into the act in the 1930s, pointing to Harden and Hirschfeld as historical enemies of German morality and diabolical conspirators against a strong, ethical nation. Without a doubt, the Eulenburg debacle hurt German Jews, just as it harmed those intrepid, forward-looking women who had begun crusading for gender equality in German society.

Sexism

The women's emancipation movement, which had been progressing rather well since the late 1800s, was portrayed as a leading contributor to the moral disintegration of society, and was, for this reason, immobilized for over a decade. The movement was dragged into the Eulenburg fiasco by opponents of feminism who saw in the scandal the chance to link the women's movement to the media's sexually explicit reporting and to lesbianism, despite the fact that feminism was unrelated to the scandal's press coverage. Lesbianism had not even been an issue either before or during the Eulenburg Affair. Nevertheless, the backlash that followed the scandal permitted foes of both feminism and lesbianism to accuse politically progressive women of hastening the decay of the empire.

Homophobia

Although optimistic historians have praised the Eulenburg Affair for making homosexuality a household topic in Germany at the time, thereby forcing the matter out of the societal closet, the reality is that it did so in a traumatic fashion. It painted same-sex love as furtive, shameful, and depraved, as something to be avoided at all costs lest one's life be ruined. As such, it did no immediate favors to gay men and women, rather, it fueled the homophobia already existent in Germany. Indeed, whereas antigay prejudice was present in German society before the scandal—Maximilian Harden had banked on it when he decided to expose Eulenburg and Moltke's amorous relationship—the public's antipathy toward gay men and lesbians escalated sharply as a consequence of the affair and impacted the homosexual populace rapidly and ruthlessly.

Authorities expanded Germany's antihomosexuality injunction to include lesbians and enlarged and fortified the law in other respects so it could yield more prosecutions. Unfortunately, it succeeded. Whereas before the scandal there was an average of 363 arrests for same-sex activities in Germany each year (1903-1907), in the wake of the affair this number rose to 542 arrests (1909-1913)—a 33 percent increase.[16] Worse still, this figure continued rising until 1918, when World War I ended and the kaiser abdicated. Curiously, in 1908 at the height of the scandal, only 282 people were apprehended—the lowest number on record—presumably because the gay citizenry was so intimidated by the hostile atmosphere surrounding the trials that it had largely gone into hiding.

Damaged, too, was Magnus Hirschfeld's organization created to fight for the repeal of the empire's antihomosexuality law. This was due mainly to Hirschfeld's own imprudent actions, most notably to his discrediting himself during the libel trials. It seems donations from wealthy, closeted gay men and lesbians plummeted 67 percent after the celebrated doctor took the stand and declared that Kuno von Moltke was gay. Either Hirschfeld's donors were worried that he might, at some point, expose their own same-sex orientations or they were simply afraid to be affiliated with the prominent activist and his group at such an uncertain, perilous time. Whatever the reason, Hirschfeld's organization suffered immensely in terms of both financial support and professional influence.

Of course, the larger gay rights movement suffered as well. Inasmuch as the quest for gay equality had been progressing steadily prior to the Eulenburg Affair, afterward it came to a virtual standstill. Since homosexuality became associated in the public mind with lechery, treachery, and extortion, it was just too dangerous for gay men and lesbians to assert their legitimacy and campaign for their rights. As for those few brave souls who did continue pushing for recognition and respect, they were, as were the small number of feminists who continued fighting for gender equality, perceived as menaces to society and were barely tolerated. The gay emancipation movement was therefore stagnant until World War I ended and the kaiser departed.

Militarism

Perhaps the most far-reaching effect of the Eulenburg Affair, however, involved the military. In the years immediately preceding the scandal, concern was growing that the empire's armed forces were losing morale and discipline, an opinion expressed in scores of newspaper articles, autobiographical accounts, and works of fiction. This perception was deeply disturbing, especially considering Germany's history of touting itself as a leading European power. Distressing, too, were the twenty-odd court-martials that had taken place shortly before the Eulenburg Affair, as well as the growing number of resignations and suicides of military personnel. The exquisitely timed Eulenburg trials, which implicated a number of military officers in same-sex activities and summoned enlisted men as witnesses, seemed to confirm society's fears. The state of the military became intensely troubling to those in power, and troubling as well to a substantial share of the public. Many parents became unwilling to let their sons join the army.

Naturally, this focus on the military directly impacted Kaiser Wilhelm II. It seems that Harden's calculated smear of the kaiser, via Eulenburg, Moltke, and others, worked only too well. As the militant publisher had hoped, in the short term the scandal caused the public to view the kaiser as deficient in character and courage. Harden was not prepared for its long-term effects, however. The kaiser, it turns out, did not become the political lame duck as anticipated, but instead became steadily more confrontive in an effort to change the public perception of himself and his military as being passive and weak. This increase in aggressiveness was easy for him to accomplish, since he had fewer companions such as Philipp Eulenburg to serve as mollifying influences in his life, people who could help contain his militaristic tendencies. Certainly, the ambitious kaiser, by all accounts, needed the presence of such calming influences. He had always required the guidance of composed, rational individuals, advisors whose heads were cooler than his own. Maximilian Harden finally came to recognize this truth. Several years after the scandal ended, the publisher confided to a colleague that only after he had driven away Eulenburg and other gay comrades from the kaiser's court did he realize that these men had, in fact, been exerting a pacifying effect, that without them the kaiser quickly became imperialistic and unrestrained. Saying he regretted having launched the scandal, Harden admitted it had been the most profound political mistake of his life. Several historians, American, French, and British, have since agreed with his assessment. The consensus is that the removal of Philipp Eulenburg and other such companions from the kaiser's side, in conjunction with the military's diminishing reputation, prompted crucial changes in German foreign policy and led to a sharp increase in militarism, a chain of events that some say contributed to the outbreak of World War I.

From the foregoing, it is evident that the Eulenburg Affair was destructive on several levels. It damaged the reputations, along with the health, of all the major figures drawn into it and tarnished the images of diverse segments of the German population not directly involved in the incident. Because the atmosphere surrounding the scandal allowed extremists of all stripes to come forward and scapegoat minorities, social and political progress was hindered for quite some time.

In addition, the affair permitted journalists to run wild. Unconstrained for the first time in years, and therefore highly spirited and daring, the press increasingly encroached upon the privacy of the people in the name of comprehensive reporting. The result was that many citizens, especially gay men and members of the aristocracy, found themselves at the mercy of the media.

The scandal also exposed the manner in which a judicial system may hand down faulty decisions for strictly political ends. In the Eulenburg Affair, the verdicts were most often designed to stifle the press, appease the public, or protect the reputation of the ruling class, regardless of who was right or wrong under the law. In this respect, the judiciary was as dubious as those men who perpetrated the outings.

Ultimately, the repercussions of the Eulenburg exposé expanded far and wide; little good came from the incident and much that was bad. Perhaps it is for this reason that, after the 1930s, the episode was rarely discussed publicly for the next fifty years. In the end, it seems that the Eulenburg Affair provided the German people a reason for chagrin, and proved, once again, the power of scandal.

Notes

Introduction

1. Faderman (1983, p. 65).

Chapter 1

1. Casement, in Hochschild (1999 [1998], p. 287).
2. Ibid.
3. Forbath (1977, p. 328).
4. Ibid.
5. Leopold, in Forbath (1977, p. 329).
6. Forbath (1977, p. 362).
7. Burton, in Hochschild (1999 [1998], p. 50).
8. Stanley, in Hochschild (1999 [1998], p. 49).
9. Hochschild (1999 [1998], p. 151).
10. In Forbath (1977, p. 374).
11. Hochschild (1999 [1998], p. 166).
12. In Gwynn (1931, p. 65).
13. Conrad, in Inglis (1973, p. 31).
14. Casement, in Sawyer (1997, p. 168).
15. Ibid., p. 144.
16. Ibid., p. 149.
17. Inglis (1973, p. 187).
18. Ibid., p. 194.
19. Casement, in Sawyer (1997, p. 43).
20. Ibid.
21. Ibid., p. 44.
22. Ibid., p. 117.
23. Casement, in Doerries (2000, p. 5).
24. Casement, in Inglis (1973, p. 307).
25. Ibid., p. 311.
26. Casement, in Doerries (2000, p. 205).
27. Casement, in Inglis (1973, pp. 312-313).
28. Casement, in Gwynn (1931, p. 394).
29. Toolis (1995, p. 339).
30. Smith, in Gwynn (1931, p. 409).
31. Casement, in Gwynn (1931, p. 418).
32. In Inglis (1973, p. 341).
33. Ibid., p. 359.

34. Ibid., p. 358.
35. Noyes, in Inglis (1973, p. 377).
36. Reid (1976, p. 481).
37. Kennedy (2000).
38. Dudgeon, in Burns (2000, p. 1).
39. Rowse (1977, p. 259).

Chapter 2

1. Reeves (1999, p. 206).
2. Hay (1987).
3. Ibid.
4. Ibid., p. 87.
5. Siciliano (1982 [1978], p. 40).
6. Ibid., p. 37.
7. Ibid., p. 135.
8. In Schwartz (1992, p. 221).
9. Siciliano (1982 [1978], p. 162).
10. Greene (1990, p. 23).
11. Siciliano (1982 [1978]).
12. Marcus (1986, p. 251).
13. Ibid., p. 249.
14. Ibid., p. 250.
15. Pasolini, in Greene (1990, p. 133).
16. Ibid., p. 197.
17. Siciliano (1982 [1978]).
18. Ibid., p. 285.
19. Rossellini (1995 [1987], p. 187).
20. Pasolini, in Greene (1990, p. 201).
21. Kriegsman (1977, p. B-9).
22. Huston, in Greene (1990, p. 201).
23. Arnold (1977, p. B-7).
24. Reed, in Schwartz (1992, p. 689).
25. Walsh (1995, p. 3).
26. Siciliano (1982 [1978]).
27. Ibid.
28. Pelosi, in Siciliano (1982 [1978], p. 8).
29. Ibid., p. 9.
30. In Siciliano (1982 [1978], p. 16).
31. Pasolini, in Schwartz (1992, p. 26).
32. In Siciliano (1982 [1978], p. 13).
33. Schwartz (1992, p. 677).
34. Siciliano (1982 [1978], p. 391).
35. In Schwartz (1992, p. 673).
36. Pasolini, in Schwartz (1992, p. 690).
37. Ibid., p. 662.

Chapter 3

1. Douglas, in Brittain (1969 [1963], p. 16).
2. Brittain (1969 [1963], p. 31).
3. Hall, in Souhami (1999, p. 37).
4. Hall (1990 [1928], p. 152).
5. Ibid., p. 301.
6. Hall, in Souhami (1999, p. 163).
7. Hall (1990 [1928], p. 437).
8. In Souhami (1999, pp. 188-189).
9. Ibid., p. 225.
10. In Brittain (1969 [1963], p. 92).
11. Ibid., p. 100.
12. Ibid.
13. Hall, in Brittain (1969 [1963], p. 101).
14. In Souhami (1999, p. xvii).
15. In Brittain (1969 [1963], p. 123).
16. Wallace, in Brittain (1969 [1963], p. 126).
17. Knopf, in Souhami (1999, p. 205).
18. Souhami (1999, p. 237).
19. In Brittain (1969 [1963], p. 112).

Chapter 4

1. Denny (1951, p. 1).
2. Volkman (1995).
3. In Boyle (1979, p. 56).
4. Fisher (1977, p. 27).
5. Ibid., p. 30.
6. Burgess, in Boyle (1979, p. 447).
7. Modin et al. (1994, p. 68).
8. Page et al. (1968, p. 76).
9. Fisher (1977, p. 43).
10. Modin et al. (1994, p. 86).
11 Fisher (1977, p. 45).
12. Ibid.
13. Rees (1977, p. 174).
14. Modin et al. (1994, p. 103).
15. Fisher (1977, p. 58).
16. In Deacon (1972, p. 417).
17. Modin et al. (1994, p. 96).
18. Connolly (1952, p. 1).
19. Fisher (1977, p. 69).
20. Mark Culmé-Seymour, in Page et al. (1968, p. 81).
21. Knightly (1990, p. 74).
22. Boyle (1979, pp. 158-159).
23. U.S. Atomic Energy Commission (1951).
24. Ibid.

25. Modin et al. (1994, p. 118).
26. CIA/FBI, in Boyle (1979).
27. Knightly (1990, p. 171).
28. Ibid.
29. FBI (1951, p. 2).
30. Maclean, in Fisher (1977, p. 25).
31. Colville, in Boyle (1979, p. 394).
32. "Letters received" (1951, p. 1).
33. "Commons asked to keep cool" (1951, p. 1).
34. Freidin (1951, p. 1).
35. Coulter (1951).
36. "Bucharest radio reports arrival" (1951, p. 1).
37. "Two diplomats" (1951, p. 1).
38. Ibid.
39. Noyes (1951, p. 1).
40. "American 'third man' involved" (1951, p. 1).
41. "Why did he take the spy road?" (1955, p. 1).
42. Walker (1995, p. 68).
43. Miller (1995, p. 282).
44. Ibid.
45. Ibid.
46. In Hodges (1983, p. 501).
47. Ibid., p. 507.
48. In Rovere (1996 [1959], p. 154).
49. Committee on Homosexual Offences and Prostitution (1964 [1957], p. 15).
50. Ibid., p. 221.
51. Knightly (1990, p. 265).
52. Modin et al. (1994).
53. Burgess, in Churchill (1959, p. 1).
54. "Scotland Yard set" (1962, p. 1).
55. Walker (1995, p. 285).

Chapter 5

1. In Gevisser and Cameron (1995, p. 250).
2. Nkoli, in Krouse and Berman (1995, p. 23).
3. In Krouse and Berman (1995, p. 23).
4. Nkoli, in Gevisser and Cameron (1995, p. 252).
5. In Gevisser and Cameron (1995, p. 252).
6. Bohannan and Curtin (1971).
7. Christiansen (2000, p. 1019).
8. Krouse and Berman (1995, p. xvii).
9. In Gevisser and Cameron (1995, p. 101).
10. Ibid., p. 102.
11. Isaacs and McKendrick (1992, p. 155).
12. Nkoli, in Miller (1992, p. 10).
13. "Vryburg mayor tells" (1996, p. 1).
14. Haysom (1988/1989, p. 3).

15. In Gevisser and Cameron (1995, p. 254).
16. Sampson (1987).
17. Nkoli, in Miller (1992, p. 11).
18. In Gevisser (1998, p. 1).
19. Nkoli, in Miller (1992, p. 11).
20. Miller (1992, p. 11).
21. Nkoli, in Gevisser and Cameron (1995, p. 256).
22. Molefe, in Claiborne (1988, p. A-1).
23. Lekota, in Grau (2001, p. 3).
24. International Gay and Lesbian Association (1999, p. 1).

Chapter 6

1. Franklin (1997).
2. Sinclair and Omang (1980, p. A-22).
3. "In Mariel, massive boatlift" (2000, p. A-1).
4. Fix and Gyllenhaal (1980, p. A-14).
5. Sinclair and Omang (1980, p. A-22).
6. Brown (1980, p. A-11).
7. Simons (1980, p. A-15).
8. Bethel (1993).
9. Anders, in Young (1981, p. 10).
10. Lumsden (1996, p. 35).
11. Young (1981, p. 4).
12. Lumsden (1996, p. 32).
13. Arenas (1993 [1992], pp. 50-51).
14. Young (1981, p. 17).
15. Soto (1998).
16. Raab, in Timerman (1990, pp. 57-58).
17. Soto (1998, p. 32).
18. In Yglesias (1968, p. 278).
19. Arenas (1993 [1992], p. 105).
20. Infante (November 7, 1993, p. X-3).
21. In Arenas (1993 [1992], p. 210).
22. Soto (1998, p. 32).
23. Solzhenitsyn, in Bartlett (1980, p. 895).
24. Pasternak, in Bartlett (1980, p. 816).
25. Arenas (1994 [1991], pp. 52-53).
26. In Arenas (1993 [1992], p. 271).
27. Manrique (1999, p. 65).
28. Arenas, in Manrique (1999, p. 65).
29. Ibid., p. 317.
30. Ibid.

Chapter 7

1. Miller (1995, p. 117).
2. Bismarck, in Duberman et al. (1989, p. 237).

3. Harden, in Miller (1995, p. 119).

4. Richie (1998, p. 262).

5. Steakley (1993 [1975], p. 37).

6. In Richie (1998, p. 263).

7. von Elbe, in Spencer (1995, p. 315).

8. Duberman et al. (1989).

9. Brand, in Oosterhuis and Kennedy (1991, p. 197).

10. Ibid., p. 6.

11. Steakley, in Duberman et al. (1989, p. 244).

12. Ernst, in Spencer (1995, p. 317).

13. Ernst, in Duberman et al. (1989, p. 245).

14. Eulenburg, in Miller (1995, p. 121).

15. Kaiser Wilhelm II, in Miller (1995, p. 121).

16. Miller (1995).

Bibliography

"American 'third man' involved in mystery of missing diplomats" (1951). *The Washington Star,* June 22, p. 1.

Arenas, Reinaldo (1993 [1992]). *Before Night Falls. A Memoir.* New York: Penguin Books (originally published by Tusquet Editores, S. A., Spain).

Arenas, Reinaldo (1994 [1991]). *The Assault.* New York: Penguin Books (originally published by Ediciones Universal, Miami).

Arnold, Gary (1977). "*Salo:* An oppressive swan song." *The Washington Post,* November 29, p. B-7.

Bartlett, John (1980). *Bartlett's Familiar Quotations.* Boston: Little, Brown and Co.

Bethel, Leslie (Ed.) (1993). *Cuba: A Short History.* Cambridge, England: Cambridge University Press.

Bohannan, Paul and Curtin, Philip (1971). *Africa and Africans.* Garden City, NY: Natural History Press.

Boyle, Andrew (1979). *The Climate of Treason: Five Who Spied for Russia.* London: Hutchinson of London.

Brittain, Vera (1969 [1963]). *Radclyffe Hall: A Case of Obscenity?* New York: A. S. Barnes and Company.

Brown, Warren (1980). "Reports on number of gays disputed; Cuban refugees." *The Washington Post,* July 10, p. A-11.

"Bucharest radio reports arrival of hunted diplomats in Prague: One of Europe's greatest manhunts pressed as cold trail leads from France to Italy" (1951). *The Washington Star,* June 10, p. 1.

Burns, John (2000). "Bertie Ahern." *The Sunday Times,* May 7. Accessed online June 15, 2001: <http://www.sunday-times.co.uk>.

Christiansen, Eric C. (2000). "Ending the apartheid of the closet: Sexual orientation in the South African constitutional process." *International Law and Politics,* 32 (November 2), pp. 997-1058.

Churchill, Randolph (1959). "Randolph Churchill in Moscow: Old-school-tie Burgess calls on me." *Evening Standard* (London), February 23.

Claiborne, William (1988). "Four black activists convicted of treason in South Africa." *The Washington Post,* November 19, p. A-1.

Committee on Homosexual Offences and Prostitution (1964 [1957]). *The Wolfenden Report: Report of the Committee on Homosexual Offences and Prostitution.* New York: Lancer Books.

"Commons asked to keep cool about two missing diplomats" (1951). *The Washington Post,* June 11, p. 1.

Connolly, Cyril (1952). "The missing diplomats." *Sunday Times* (London), September 21, p. 1.

Coulter, Stephen (1951). "Mystery Briton is questioned." *Sunday Chronicle* (London), June 11, p. 1.

Deacon, Richard (1972). *A History of the Russian Secret Service*. London: Frederick Muller.

Denny, Ludwell (1951). "Vanishing acts throws big scare into British: Writer sees wide repercussions even if two diplomats are found." *World Telegraph*, June 8.

Doerries, Reinhard (2000). *Prelude to the Easter Rising: Sir Roger Casement and Imperial Germany*. London: Frank Cass Publishers.

Duberman, M., Vicinus, M., and Chauncey, G. (Eds.) (1989). *Hidden from History: Reclaiming the Gay and Lesbian Past*. New York: Meridian Books.

Faderman, Lillian (1983). *Scotch Verdict: Miss Pirie and Miss Woods v. Dame Cumming Gordon*. London: Quartet Books, Ltd.

Federal Bureau of Investigation (1951). Untitled document (Re: Donald Duart MacLean/Guy Francis de Moncy Burgess), June 19, p. 1.

Fisher, John (1977). *Burgess and Maclean: A New Look at the Foreign Office Spies*. London: Book Club Associates.

Fix, Janet and Gyllenhaal, Anders (1980). "Boat forced to bring convicts and mental patients reaches Florida." *The Washington Post*, May 12, p. A-14.

Forbath, Peter (1977). *The River Congo: The Discovery, Exploration and Exploitation of the World's Most Dramatic River*. New York: Harper and Row.

Franklin, Jane (1997). *Cuba and the United States: A Chronological History*. New York/Melbourne: Ocean Press.

Freidin, Seymour (1951). "Russians hint diplomats in red hands." *New York Post*, June 11, p. 1.

Gevisser, Mark (1998). "A leading light of gay and AIDS activism in South Africa." *The Sunday Times* (South Africa), December 6. Accessed online May 5, 2001, from Behind the Mask database: <http://www.mask.org.za/Sections/Profiles/profile4.html>.

Gevisser, Mark and Cameron, Edwin (Eds.) (1995). *Defiant Desire: Gay and Lesbian Lives in South Africa*. London: Routledge.

Grau, Rawley (2001). "Who was Simon Nkoli?" *Daily Mail and Guardian*, January 3. Accessed online May 5, 2001, from Q database: <http://www.q.co.za/culture/01features/010103-nkoli.htm>.

Greene, Naomi (1990). *Pier Paolo Pasolini: Cinema As Heresy*. Princeton: Princeton University Press.

Gwynn, Denis (1931). *Traitor or Patriot: The Life and Death of Roger Casement*. London/New York: Jonathan Cape and Harrison Smith.

Hall, Radclyffe (1990 [1928]). *The Well of Loneliness*. New York: Anchor Books.

Hay, James (1987). *Popular Film Culture in Fascist Italy: The Passing of the Rex*. Bloomington: Indiana University Press.

Haysom, Nicholas (1988/1989). "Order without law." *South African Review of Books,* December/January. Accessed online May 15, 2001, from the University of Ulm database: <http://www.uniulm.de/~rturrell/antho4html/Haysom.html>.

Hochschild, Adam (1999 [1998]). *King Leopold's Ghost: A Story of Greed, Terror, and Heroism in Colonial Africa.* New York: Mariner Books (originally published by Houghton Mifflin, New York).

Hodges, Andrew (1983). *Alan Turing: The Enigma.* New York: Touchstone (Simon and Schuster).

Infante, G. Cabrera (1993). "Journey to the end of the night." *The Washington Post,* November 7, p. X-3.

Inglis, Brian (1973). *Roger Casement: The Biography of a Patriot Who Lived for England, Died for Ireland.* New York: Harcourt Brace Jovanovich.

"In Mariel, Massive Boatlift a National Embarrassment" (2000). *Miami Herald,* April 21, p. 1-A.

International Lesbian and Gay Association (1999). "We mourn Simon Nkoli" (press release). Accessed online May 5, 2001, from International Lesbian and Gay Association database: <http://www.ilga.org>.

Isaacs, Gordon and McKendrick, Brian (1992). *Male Homosexuality in South Africa: Identity Formation, Culture, and Crisis.* Cape Town, South Africa: Oxford University Press.

Kennedy, Kieran (2000). "Who Framed Roger Casement?" *Lingua Franca,* November, pp. 44-53.

Knightly, Phillip (1990). *The Master Spy: The Story of Kim Philby.* New York: Vintage Books.

Kriegsman, Alan (1977). "The obsession of the New York Film Festival." *The Washington Post,* October 4, B-9.

Krouse, Matthew and Berman, Kim (1995). *The Invisible Ghetto: Lesbian and Gay Writing from South Africa.* London: Gay Men's Press.

"Letters received from missing diplomats" (1951). *Daily Telegraph,* June 8, p. 1.

Lumsden, Ian (1996). *Machos, Maricones, and Gays: Cuba and Homosexuality.* Philadelphia: Temple University Press.

Manrique, Jaime (1999). *Eminent Maricones: Arenas, Lorca, Puig, and Me.* Madison, WI: University of Wisconsin Press.

Marcus, Millicent (1986). *Italian Film in the Light of Neorealism.* Princeton: Princeton University Press.

Miller, Neil (1992). *Out in the World: Gay and Lesbian Life from Buenos Aires to Bangkok.* New York: Random House.

Miller, Neil (1995). *Out of the Past: Gay and Lesbian History from 1869 to the Present.* New York: Vintage Books.

Modin, Yuri, Deniau, Jean-Charles, and Aguieszka, Ziarek (1994). *My Five Cambridge Friends: Burgess, Maclean, Philby, Blunt, and Cairncross by Their KGB Controller.* New York: Farrar, Straus and Giroux.

Noyes, Newbold (1951). "Two runaway diplomats create one of the world's great mystery stories." *The Washington Star,* June 17, p. 1.

Oosterhuis, Harry and Kennedy, Hubert (Eds.) (1991). *Homosexuality and Male Bonding in Pre-Nazi Germany.* Binghamton, NY: The Haworth Press.

Page, Bruce, Leitch, David, and Knightly, Phillip (1968*). Philby: The Spy Who Betrayed a Generation.* London: André Deutsch, Ltd.

Rees, Goronwy (1977). *A Chapter of Accidents.* London: Chatto and Windus.

Reeves, Nicholas (1999). *The Power of Film Propaganda: Myth of Reality?* London: Cassell.

Reid, Benjamin L. (1976). *The Lives of Roger Casement.* New Haven: Yale University Press.

Richie, Alexandra (1998). *Faust's Metropolis: A History of Berlin.* New York: Carroll and Graf.

Rossellini, Roberto (1995 [1987]). *My Method: Writings and Interviews.* New York: Marsilio Publishing (originally published by Marsilio Editori, Milan, Italy).

Rovere, Richard (1996 [1959]). *Senator Joe McCarthy.* Berkeley: University of California Press (originally published by Harcourt Brace Jovanovich, New York).

Rowse, A. L. (1977). *Homosexuals in History: A Study of Ambivalence in Society, Literature and the Arts.* New York: Carroll and Graf.

Sampson, Anthony (1987). *Black and Gold: Tycoons, Revolutionaries and Apartheid.* Kent, England: Coronet Books (Hodder and Stoughton).

Sawyer, Roger (Ed.) (1997). *Roger Casement's Diaries: 1910, the Black and the White.* London: Pimlico (Random House).

Schwartz, Barth (1992). *Pasolini Requiem.* New York: Pantheon Books.

"Scotland Yard set if defectors show" (1962). *The Washington Post,* April 18, p. 1.

Siciliano, Enzo (1982 [1978]). *Pasolini: A Biography.* New York: Random House (originally published by Rizzoli Editore, Milan).

Simons, Marlise (1980). "Some residents unwittingly swept into political fury." *The Washington Post,* May 12, p. A-15.

Sinclair, Ward and Omang, Joanne (1980). "U. S. cracks down on refugee boats." *The Washington Post,* April 26, p. A-22.

Soto, Francisco (1998). *Reinaldo Arenas* (World Author Series). New York: Twayne Publishers (Simon and Schuster/Macmillan).

Souhami, Diana (1999). *The Trials of Radclyffe Hall.* New York: Doubleday.

Spencer, Colin (1995). *Homosexuality in History.* New York: Harcourt, Brace and Co.

Steakley, James D. (1993 [1975]). *The Homosexual Emancipation Movement in Germany.* Salem, NH: Ayers Company Publishers, Inc.

Timerman, Jacob (1990). *Cuba: A Journey.* New York: Alfred Knopf.

Toolis, Kevin (1995). *Rebel Hearts: Journeys Within the IRA's Soul.* New York: St. Martin's Press.

"Two diplomats' whereabouts still a mystery" (1951) *The Washington Post,* October 20, p. 1.

U.S. Atomic Energy Commission (1951). Untitled document, July 10.

Volkman, Ernest (1995). *Espionage: The Greatest Spy Operations of the 20th Century.* New York: John Wiley and Sons.

"Vryburg mayor tells Truth Commission of assault, torture" (1996). *South African Press Association,* July 9. Accessed online May 15, 2001, from Truth and Reconciliation Committee database: <http://www.anc.org.za/anc/newsbrief/1996/news0710>.

Walker, Martin (1995). *The Cold War: A History.* New York: Henry Holt (Owl Books).

Walsh, David (November 20, 1995). "Why was Pasolini murdered? A view of *Pasolini, an Italian Crime.*" Accessed online June 16, 2001 from World Socialist Web Site: <http://www.wsws.org>.

"Why did he take the spy road? The answer lies in a nation's past, with a warning for today's generation" (1955). *Daily Mail* (London), September 28, pp. 22-23.

Yglesias, Jose (1968). *In the Fist of the Revolution: Life in a Cuban Country Town.* New York: Vintage Books.

Young, Allen (1981). *Gays Under the Cuban Revolution.* San Francisco: Grey Fox Press.

Index

SPECIAL 25%-OFF DISCOUNT!
Order a copy of this book with this form or online at:
http://www.haworthpressinc.com/store/product.asp?sku=4702

SCANDAL
Infamous Gay Controversies of the Twentieth Century

_____in hardbound at $26.21 (regularly $34.95) (ISBN: 1-56023-411-3)

_____in softbound at $14.96 (regularly $19.95) (ISBN: 1-56023-412-1)

Or order online and use Code HEC25 in the shopping cart.

COST OF BOOKS_____

OUTSIDE US/CANADA/
MEXICO: ADD 20%_____

POSTAGE & HANDLING_____
*(US: $5.00 for first book & $2.00
for each additional book)
Outside US: $6.00 for first book
& $2.00 for each additional book)*

SUBTOTAL_____

IN CANADA: ADD 7% GST_____

STATE TAX_____
*(NY, OH & MN residents, please
add appropriate local sales tax)*

FINAL TOTAL_____
*(If paying in Canadian funds,
convert using the current
exchange rate, UNESCO
coupons welcome)*

☐ **BILL ME LATER:** ($5 service charge will be added)
(Bill-me option is good on US/Canada/Mexico orders only;
not good to jobbers, wholesalers, or subscription agencies.)

☐ Check here if billing address is different from
shipping address and attach purchase order and
billing address information.

Signature_____

☐ **PAYMENT ENCLOSED: $_____**

☐ **PLEASE CHARGE TO MY CREDIT CARD.**

☐ Visa ☐ MasterCard ☐ AmEx ☐ Discover
☐ Diner's Club ☐ Eurocard ☐ JCB

Account # _____

Exp. Date_____

Signature_____

Prices in US dollars and subject to change without notice.

NAME_____

INSTITUTION_____

ADDRESS_____

CITY_____

STATE/ZIP_____

COUNTRY_____ COUNTY (NY residents only)_____

TEL_____ FAX_____

E-MAIL_____

May we use your e-mail address for confirmations and other types of information? ☐ Yes ☐ No
We appreciate receiving your e-mail address and fax number. Haworth would like to e-mail or fax special
discount offers to you, as a preferred customer. **We will never share, rent, or exchange your e-mail address
or fax number.** We regard such actions as an invasion of your privacy.

Order From Your Local Bookstore or Directly From
The Haworth Press, Inc.
10 Alice Street, Binghamton, New York 13904-1580 • USA
TELEPHONE: 1-800-HAWORTH (1-800-429-6784) / Outside US/Canada: (607) 722-5857
FAX: 1-800-895-0582 / Outside US/Canada: (607) 722-6362
E-mailto: getinfo@haworthpressinc.com
PLEASE PHOTOCOPY THIS FORM FOR YOUR PERSONAL USE.
http://www.HaworthPress.com   BOF02